PROFESSIONAL
FOOTBALL
PLAYER

First published in August 2018

British Library Cataloguing in Publication Data

A catalogue record for this book is available from the British Library.

ISBN: 978 1 78521 028 0

Library of Congress catalog card no. 2017933527

Published by Haynes Publishing,
Sparkford, Yeovil, Somerset BA22 7JJ, UK
Tel: 01963 440635
Int. tel: +44 1963 440635
Website: www.haynes.com

Haynes North America Inc.
861 Lawrence Drive, Newbury Park,
California 91320, USA

Designed by Razor Creative Ltd

Printed and bound in Malaysia

PROFESSIONAL FOOTBALL PLAYER

Owners' Workshop Manual

A guide to owning, managing and maintaining a top football player

00

CONTENTS

01

DREAM A LITTLE DREAM...

It's every impressionable schoolkid's dream – to be a professional footballer. And, the brutal reality is that, from a young age, for many it's not just about playing the game, but enjoying the trappings of success. At first, it's about playing for a proper club and emulating childhood heroes, playing for Manchester United, Liverpool, Chelsea, Arsenal, Tottenham, Manchester City, or any big team. Then come the fantasies about wealth, the multi-million-pound contract, fast cars, big houses, and, as those starry-eyed boys grow into young men, beautiful women.

It's the lifestyle of a Premier League superstar. And all of the glamour that goes with it. It's what so many male football fans wanted to be once upon a time. They were those kids in the playground, kicking a football around, dreaming of stardom. That was, of course, until most realised that they were not anywhere near good enough to make it. But that doesn't necessarily mean a career in football ends there. . .

A bad name in the game

If someone is not good enough as a player, then the next best thing is to work in football, which has become one of the world's biggest and most high-profile leisure industries.

That could be as a journalist, working in TV and the wider media. There are opportunities to try to make it within the game – working for a club or a big-name sponsor, for example. There are plenty of openings for ambitious young men and women in these fields.

And there's another option that might – just might – be available. And that's working as a football agent. Or an 'intermediary' as they're all apparently

known now. Or, as some would have it, a stain upon the game.

There are plenty of people in the sport who cannot abide agents. They are often painted in the newspapers as the lowest of the low – usually by those journalists who the agents have not managed to get on their side – or at least not just yet. These hacks label agents as greedy, troublesome and the enemy of the game.

It's not much better in the boardroom. The chief executives and chairmen of clubs don't like agents unless they're either on the payroll or handed them the hottest football talent in an incredible deal.

Agents are more unpopular than estate agents, journalists, and traffic wardens put together.

If you aren't good enough on the pitch, then a career in the media connected to football could keep your hand in. (Shutterstock)

▶ WHAT THE AGENT SAID

All agents great and small

Danny Ings, who shares holidays with his agent. (Shutterstock)

The clichéd image of an agent is just that – a cliché. There are some who of course live up to the billing: cockney wide boys who drive flash cars, wear over-the-top suits, drip with gold jewellery and are forever talking very loudly into mobile phones. But they are a declining and outdated minority.

Agents come in all shapes and sizes and from all kinds of backgrounds. It's a complete cross section of society. Former players, failed players, failed scouts, coaches. Cab drivers. Nightclub promoters. DJs. Even vacuum cleaner salesmen.

In a roomful of football agents there will be individuals with very different back stories, approaches, and characters. Some will be former players. Paul Stretford is the renowned agent associated with amongst others, Wayne Rooney and is known for being a former vacuum cleaner salesman. Jonathan Barnett was instrumental in Gareth

Former salesman of vacuum cleaners and agent to Wayne Rooney, Paul Stretford. (Getty)

Bale's transfer to Real Madrid. Barnett was one of the first agents to appear in football, having originally been the agent for former West Indies batsman Brian Lara.

But all agents have the same thing in common – they have an ability to get to know footballers. A lot of fathers and brothers end up in the business, and there's a whole new breed of agents under the intermediary system. That has encouraged family members to try and muscle in. Now, more than ever, families have tried to become involved in managing the affairs and being agents to get a slice of the cake and the rewards that go with it.

Thanks to decisions by the governing bodies, the world of football agency is largely unregulated. The relaxation of the rules has completely changed things and now all kinds of people can become involved in a player's career.

One of the first rules of business is to not make things too personal. But the nature of an agent – player relationship means that often, and over time, close friendships do develop. It's not about becoming best mates, but trust and friendship is always good for the relationship.

To take the example of Dele Alli: why would he think anything but good of the Segals? Rob had taken the player from MK Dons to Tottenham, to the England squad. That's pretty exceptional, and builds rapport.

The friendship evolves. It can help build an element of loyalty to a certain degree. When a player trusts an agent and they can talk about things with honesty, it fosters good relationships. It can hinder as well, but it helps things run smoothly if the player and his representative get to know each other well.

Sometimes the accusation is that agents are too close and lose their objectivity. But these days the modern agent is more of a brother than just an adviser. The best agents will make sure their client is focused both on and off the pitch. Increasingly, managers will say that if he asks a player to do something, the player will say: 'I'll have to ask my agent.' Back in the day, they used to ask their dad.

'Blood sucking leeches' is one of the nicer descriptions I've heard about football agents. Except some of them are pretty likable once people get to know them. And players, naturally, like them a whole lot more if their agent gets them a big fat contract, a similarly rewarding boot deal, and oh-so lucrative image rights.

The simple fact is it is the agents who can put kids on the road to stardom. They play a key role in how the sport functions. As will be explained through the pages of this book, agents wield so much power in a footballer's career.

The agents can decide whether a player makes it by negotiating the right deal, taking them to the right club and giving them the right advice. So what follows is the inside story, taking a close look at their influence throughout the game and the business.

Keeping it tight

The personal relationships between players and their agents are fundamental to how effective the business relationship can be. Danny Ings and Charlie Austin have been very tight with their agent David Threlfall. He's even been on holiday with Danny and is godfather to Charlie's child. That keeps people 'tight'; the agent, even if he works for an agency with multiple staff, is essentially a one-man-band and that one-to-one relationship with his client breeds trust. It's no guarantee of loyalty but makes it less likely that the agent would 'do the dirty' on someone and betray a person who is, basically, a friend.

Hunger games

There is not one thing – one quality – which makes someone an agent or more importantly makes someone a good agent.

Agents have all got different qualities. Some have a better eye for a player, some

School footballers can provide a good starting point for an aspiring agent.
(Shutterstock)

are better businessmen, or a negotiator. Yet all have a hunger to succeed. That hunger is a must, a 'given'. Otherwise they will never make it in what is a cut-throat business.

Agents start out in the sport differently. But the path into the business of football is a familiar one. Usually it's due to growing up watching, playing or going to football, and developing a love for the game. There is a common misconception that agents are not football fans. This is not true. While there are examples of agents who have no interest in or actual knowledge of the sport whatsoever, seeing only the opportunity to make money, most agents get into the game initially because they have some understanding of it based on their own interest in the sport.

There are agents who know more about the clubs they support than the biggest fans. Quite often they find themselves working in the industry through previous connections. They might have become mates with the best footballer at school, and enter the sport as that friend's own career develops.

The path to the top

Here is one scenario from how it often used to work. An agent of the future made friends with the school star. The player who was head and shoulders ahead of the rest. Strong, skilful, the centre-forward for the first team.

Our aspiring agent could play a bit, too. He was in the same school team,

and like everyone else, looked up to the best player. They went to school together, played in the same team together, went down the park for a kick-about.

They both dreamed of making it as professional footballers. The best kids ended up playing for the best teams in the area from a young age. But others, the ones who weren't quite as good, found themselves being quickly left behind.

Say this happened in Manchester. Everyone at a local school in the area is a mad United or City fan. The best kids from the school teams would go to United or City. Anything else was seen as being second best. There were really only two teams, but just the one dream: make it as a pro with one of the big clubs.

The local schoolboy star got invited to go and train with one of those top clubs. He played for the youth teams, came through the academy and looked like being one of the very, *very* few who might make it into the first team. Suddenly he was being talked about as a future England international. His mates from school who gave up playing went and watched him. He was a star in the making and, even before he had broken through, he'd had a little entourage hanging round him.

'Can I represent you?'

While the school's star turn progressed with his football career, his mates went on with their studies, got office jobs, working nine to five and living out old fantasies each weekend going to watch games rather than play in them.

11

One lad was living the dream – the others were clinging onto it.

But that young player didn't have an agent. Suddenly dozens of agents were swarming around him. 'Can I represent you?' they would ask. Each time he got in the first-team squad, the players' lounge after the game would be full of agents trying to sign him up. He took his friends into the suite with him because he trusted them from the old days and liked to keep his mates around him. One in particular.

Those agents were handing out business cards, offering to get him boots, a new contract and promising him the world. He was not that interested, and batted them away, pushing them onto his mate. 'Talk to him, he's with me,' he'd say, before going back to the bar.

In business

The kid's career was taking off. He was with the first team squad most weeks, making it onto the bench and, after a hot streak in the reserves, he finally got a first-team start. As more and more agents got his number, suddenly he realised he needed an agent.

Then it dawned on his mates or one of the hangers-on. Or maybe that old friend from back in the school team. 'I could do that,' he would think. And that's how it often starts. It's how it still starts for a lot of agents.

They know a player, they think they can do a good job for their mate and suddenly they're in business.

'Get lucky'

It's interesting to look at the background of many of the top agents. Some were decent players themselves, with solid careers. They didn't need to be spectacular, they were more the reliable 'journeymen'. But then injuries cut short their playing days. Or it could be they weren't quite good enough, and didn't earn enough, so they needed to do something for a living when they retired as a player. But either way by then they've established contacts in the game. And in the agent game, it's all about contacts.

For a former player who has been in the sport and had a substantial taste of it, it's common to want to stay in the business. Many find even if they weren't good enough to be a player that they wanted to be the next best thing: a football agent.

Many become wealthier as football agents than they could ever imagine as run-of-the-mill players. Some represent internationals, big-name stars, and earn millions.

They may be lucky because they used to be players, and have the opportunity to exploit that connection with other players: one big agent was panicking about what to do next after getting injured as a teenager, when he suddenly found out he was related to a young rising star. He used that connection to embark on a career in agency.

An agent has got to have some luck to make it in this game. But only a liar would try to kid anyone that's the only quality needed to make it big.

Hard graft

Agents and footballers have to work for their money. That might come as a shock to many, not to say make them laugh. But the reality is it's not as easy as some people would have outsiders believe. The jealous fans looking on will think it's easy. It really isn't.

Players need talent, invariably a good agent, and a huge slice of luck to make the grade. But hard work is essential for both player and agent.

A few players prove to be brighter than the agents think. But not many agents are at an advantage when it comes to business. Some have done their A Levels, got a degree and, most importantly, have real-world, street-level life experience.

So they make it into football representation. They get an office, get in with a top agent and start out on a new career to take a footballer to the very top.

Meanwhile, some of the players don't have so much luck as their more successful peers. They get injured, suffer serious knee injuries, don't make it as big as everyone thought, and drift out of the game with half-a-dozen first team appearances under their belt – if they are lucky. Some of the most talented players in football don't make it. It's an early lesson in the heartbreak, tough breaks and cruel lessons in this world. And agents learn those lessons well.

Tried and tested

One of the first things agents have to do is to take the agent's exam. Before that, aspiring agents had to pay a £50,000 bond to FIFA. Many wouldn't have stood a chance if they hadn't scrapped paying the bond.

Agents should be able to spot good talent, but a little piece of luck helps along the way.
(Shutterstock)

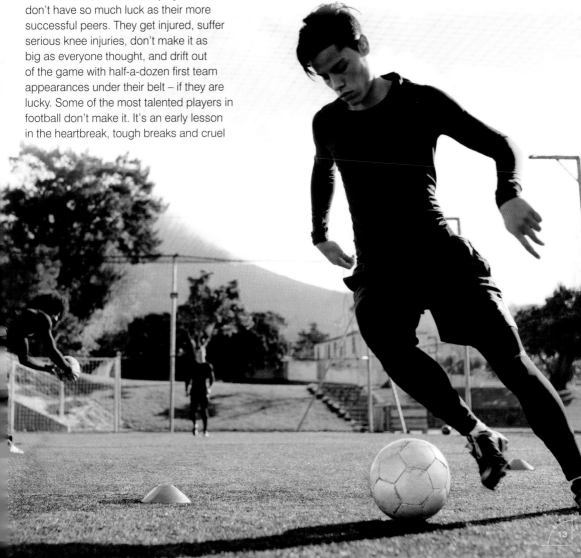

If an agent did the exam when it was first introduced in 2002, there were less than 100 agents back then. Some passed it easily, found it very easy and couldn't understand why many people failed it. There were so many unlicensed agents who remained unlicensed until they scrapped the licence system. Why? Because they couldn't pass the exam.

It wasn't difficult. If an agent did the revision and homework then it was not hard. It was multiple choice, had 20 questions, different topics from tax, image rights and contracts.

An agent could sit the exam at various places, notably at Wembley, but also at other stadia, such as Hillsborough. Taking the test was like being back at school, sitting in a conference room, desk in front of the 'students', pen and paper in hand. It was strange how many people had to retake it. This led to some suspecting that it was designed to stop too many people passing it, or at least weeding out those who didn't study and do their homework.

An agent could take it twice and then had to wait a whole year before taking it again. A lot of people thought that they could just turn up, and simply rely on the assumption that they knew everything there was to know about football.

But if they couldn't even answer a few multiple choice questions, it exposed them as not being up to the job.

By the time the licence system was repealed in April 2015, there were hundreds of agents. After the agent-licensing system was scrapped, there were suddenly 1,200 'intermediaries'; some trying to make a fast buck, some trying to get their players to the top and others still trying to live out their dreams of being a football agent.

Snobbery

There was always a lot of snobbery about licensed agents and non-licensed agents, and that has carried over into the unlicensed system. That said, it makes sense that a person should be properly qualified to deal with multi-million-pound deals. After all, that person is representing a player, looking out for his career and his best interests.

The addiction

Once a person starts to work in football, the die is cast. It's addictive. There is a buzz to being in the business. The phone never stops ringing; it is possible to work for 24 hours non-stop.

Whether for a player or someone working away from the pitch, this is an industry that never stops. Football people never have a moment when they are not involved in football. For the players it's thinking about the best move, gossiping

💬 WHAT THE AGENT SAID

BEFORE

- Agents would have to pass an exam
- There would only be just over 500 licensed agents in the UK – that trebled with the new rules
- The biggest problem was that only around 30 per cent of deals were done by licensed agents. The FA took a 'if you can't beat them, join them' approach towards agents in an attempt to clamp down

AFTER

- Pay a £500 bond
- Pass a test of good character and reputation
- Agents become known as intermediaries
- Players can only sign up for a two-year representation contract
- No licence required – but must register with FA

about team mates, what managers are doing, planning nights out with teammates, being part of the glamorous, celebrity world, or trying to get through the tough times, the drama, and the intense pressure of being a professional sportsperson.

Football is like a soap opera, or an addictive merry-go-round – players, agents, managers and all kinds of others never want to get off.

There's no set path, there's no right way and no wrong way. But, in the final analysis, people are in it to make money, and look after number one.

An agent doesn't even need the biggest or the best players. There are players getting £20,000-a-week in the Championship. Their agents don't need to have five Raheem Sterlings because if they have got five Championship players together they can be just as lucrative.

And the great thing is that they move more often. That's a great business and will earn an agent a lot of money.

Some agents are only interested in ten Championship players. They will earn £200,000 for every Championship deal. Get ten of those and that's £2m. Nice work if you can get it. It doesn't always pay to get the top players, work with the top clubs and aim to be in on the big deals, because there is potential for high earnings from work lower down the scale. Arguably, it's a better and more reliable business plan.

A piece of the action

From the players to the agents, the parents to the chairman: everybody wants a piece of the action.

This should not obscure the fact that there are very good agents, who always put the player first and will go to incredible lengths to get them to the best club, delivering the best contract and the best commercial deals.

But some of those same agents would also sell their own grandmother to get a good deal for their player – and of course the big, fat commission.

Cloak and dagger

The buzz is getting a good deal done, a deal over the line or a transfer completed on deadline day. That's the thing about this business – the buzz comes from a good

Agenting can be rewarding, lucrative and ruthless.
(Shutterstock)

deal because it's good for the player, and there's nothing better than getting that deal done.

But so many people want to get in the way. So many people want to get a slice of the pie and so there is rarely a straightforward deal in this business.

It can be cloak and dagger. There are so many twists and turns, it can be incredibly stressful and full of hassle. It can be very dispiriting and difficult, especially if someone is deceitful. With time, it gets easier. Agents become more philosophical. Yet the sucker punches are never easy to take.

The way the industry has gone, footballers have become far less genuine and nice to deal with. Yet the thrill of working in football remains. It's still about having the ability to have a positive effect on someone's career and the hope to see him one day playing at the highest level. That's the buzz and the moment an agent loses that is the moment the money takes over. The money has always come second for many. Again, that might sound laughable. but it's true.

The greed game

Families and relations can cause major headaches and problems. They can get so greedy – even when the player is at a young age.

An agent may try telling them that the money comes second – but too many simply won't believe it. There are so many

cases where a player's career has been ruined by families asking too much, or by going to the wrong club for a bit more money and then blowing the lot by making the wrong career choice.

It should not all be about greed. It should be about the buzz of that first professional contract. There's also a huge satisfaction for relatives and agents that comes from sitting in the stand and seeing 'their' player cross the white line and play in the Premier League for the first time.

That should be the biggest achievement of all – all those years, all those training sessions, the good times, the setbacks – when the player finally makes it as a professional footballer.

Threats, lies and deceit

A few years ago most people in the game would probably say it used to be far more enjoyable. It was fun, a bit more innocent and everyone was in it for the love of the game.

Now, there is more pressure, it's tougher and far harder. To a large extent the rewards on offer explain why it can be so dog-eat-dog out there.

Everyone in the game will say that they don't enjoy it so much anymore. Deals are harder, players are more difficult to find and it's getting even tougher for the player to break through and make it into the first team – let alone reach the top.

Why? There are several reasons. The agents' world hadn't become what it is now. It's become like a world full of gangsters. People threatening others on a regular basis. Everyone is always sniping. It's completely overrun with too many agents and representatives, and so it's overcrowded. And as for the lies . . . that's what many cannot abide.

Players are not very bright, frankly. They get drawn into a web of lies and deceit by agents. They fall for it, like some naïve fool being wooed by sweet nothings. They leave a good agent and go to another who might not be so good.

There are plenty of stories where players fall for all the patter. 'I'll get you a move to the Premier League,' is typical. So the player signs for another agent. But then they don't get the player that move to the Premier League. It can cost a footballer hundreds of thousands of pounds in lost earnings, bonuses and signing-on fees.

That wouldn't have happened 10 years ago. It's pure greed in the modern game. When there are too many agents jumping in on deals, such problems tend to happen. Deals go badly wrong whereas 10 or 15 years ago, when there were fewer agents, there was much less chance of that happening.

For example, with a standard, and not particularly big, deal with a player moving from a Championship club to the Premier League, there are probably between 10 and 15 agents trying to jump in on the negotiations. That's at the very least. But that's also standard.

The word goes round, people gossip, hear about the deal and try to get involved. Other agents will ring the player, say they've got a club involved, the club wants to sign them, whatever is necessary to spark or maintain interest and get them involved. Every agent thinks they can break the relationship between the player and their existing agent and offer incentives to sign with them. Money, gifts, deals, promises. People will jump on it and see nothing wrong with doing that. They will just chance their luck.

The end of loyalty

If any doubt remains about how cut-throat the agent game is, here's a story that shows just how ruthless – and chaotic – it can be.

For example, with one run-of-the-mill deal in January 2016, a player moved from a Championship club to the Premier League. Depending on who you speak to, there are three different versions of who did that deal. It's not entirely clear who the agent actually was in the end because so many others tried to jump in. Sometimes so many agents will try to get involved and make some money that the deal breaks down. About three agents all claim they did the deal, got paid and that's not unusual for the most straightforward of deals.

So many players now are not loyal because the loyalty has gone out of the game. And that applies to agents as well. As soon as the player hasn't got a club or a contract, then agents will suddenly start ignoring their calls. They don't even want to talk to them. The cash cow has gone and they don't want to know anymore. That's the brutal reality of this world.

In terms of the life cycle of a player, most stay with an agent from 16 to 21 and then they start getting rich, doing well and get a bit greedy. They get offered so much more and that's when the issues start.

And when those issues start, the greed, money and demands tend to get completely out of hand.

That's reflective of this business: there are very few people who can be trusted. Whether it's other agents tapping up players, the player ignoring calls or texts because he's signing for someone else, or someone trying to swndle someone else out of a few quid. It's a dog-eat-dog business.

02

LAW OF THE PLAYGROUND

Footballers are often not the sharpest tools in the box. Yet they are forever playing games of one-upmanship. The dressing room can be an unforgiving environment, and a pretty unsavoury one at that. They are the kind of places in which sexist, racist and too often bullying behaviour can thrive. They are home to an unwritten law: it's all about finding a weakness among teammates, and then exploiting that weakness. All because footballers are interested in one-upmanship; in being able to prove, in their minds at least, that they are 'better' than their peers.

If a player walks into a dressing room with a £4,000 Rolex, the next day, a teammate will be looking to buy one worth £6,000. If one player drives into the training ground in a brand new Ferrari California, someone else will turn up the next day in a Bugatti Veyron.

This obviously happens at the top levels where established players are earning fortunes. But long before then, at 14 to 18, players are playing the same kind of one-upmanship games. At that age it's all about boots. Kids will message agents on Twitter or Instagram begging for boots. One youngster might send a message in which he says, 'I'm not sure if I want an agent, but I do want a boot deal.

Get me those boots and then I will sign with you tomorrow.'

From 18 to 20 the competition revolves around cars, then it becomes watches, houses and luxury properties as the players become older.

If an agent manages to supply one young player with the latest boots – it could be Nike Hypervenom one minute until adidas come out with their latest design – then the player will show off to all of his mates. He will, inevitably, brag that 'my agent got them for me'. It is basic showing off, and one-upmanship at such a young age. It's dog-eat-dog and almost always revolves around money, wealth and greed.

Expensive cars go with the territory when it comes to one-upmanship in the dressing room.
(Shutterstock)

19

AWAY

Bigger. Better. Banter

Dressing room banter revolves around who is better – and not always about who is the better player. Better boots, watch, deal – whatever it is, it's got to be *better*. Players will inevitably lie to each other about how much they earn. This has equally inevitable knock-on effects, as players who believe others are earning more than them will immediately call their agent, complaining that his teammate has got a better contract.

The conversation can pan out like this:

'I was on the coach and so-and-so just told me he's on £2,000-a-week. Why am I only on £1,400? Why is he earning more than me?'

The agent will tell his client that is not true, to which the aggrieved player responds, 'Why has he said that then?'

'Because he's lying to you,' answers the agent.

It is absolute nonsense, comical even. Players are naïve and easily fooled. The distortions of what is true are juvenile. But that kind of conversation throws up all kinds of issues. The player is unhappy, and now the agent and, ultimately, the club have got a problem. All because of one-upmanship.

This kind of problem becomes particularly acute when players are called

those struggles are common knowledge and make for salacious front-page reading. Kenny Sansom, a former England international and an Arsenal legend, has had very public exposures of his alcoholism and financial problems, for example. But Sansom never earned a fraction of what young players do today. It's a gap of millions – literally and symbolically in terms of how far apart their lives are.

The incomes of modern players and what they do with their money are extraordinary. It's a whole new world of wealth and show business that older former players simply would not recognise.

There is a perception that some players earn so much money they do not know what to do with it. The former Liverpool and Arsenal player Jermaine Pennant was accused of forgetting he had a Porsche that he had left in a car park in Spain when he played for Real Zaragoza. He denied it, but that didn't stop the idea that he had more money than sense.

In reality, Pennant has done very well, overcoming what was a very challenging upbringing in a tough environment but working hard to make a career for himself in football – and a lucrative one at that. But the mud sticks.

Fault lines

It could be argued that footballers deserve some sympathy. They don't set out to become millionaires but live with a sense of responsibility and profile that other wealthy people are not bound to. Football throws young men in the deep end of fame and celebrity, and all the problems that can come with it.

But if a player decides to spend, spend, spend and waste his fortune, is that football's fault? Or is it down to the

Who is the better footballer – who has the best boots and earns the most wages, can form some of the player banter. (Getty)

up for national sides. Players from one club will be told by players at another how much more they are earning. Agents will have to step in and reassure their players this is not the case, but the problem now will not go away. It stems from a school playground mentality.

The haves and have-nots

In the modern-day game at the elite level, any player who retires after a good Premier League career really should not have to work again.

Of course, there are players who struggle after they retire. The stories of

player? Perhaps the players' union, the Professional Footballers' Association, should have more of an input. An agent can only do so much, and there has to be a realisation from the player himself to think about his long-term future. Players are told about the wisdom of pensions, and making plans for life after football, but if, as is often the case, they are unwilling to listen, how much can an agent or indeed a union do?

There has to be a little bit of responsibility. The agent can only tell a player 'you're a grown man now, mate' so many times before it's too late.

Made for life

Those who are sensible or at least not too reckless who have played at the highest level for a few years in the last few seasons are made. It doesn't matter if they don't work for another 50 years because they'll have enough money.

For many, that money will be coming out of their ears. Increasingly that's the future for players who have ridden the Premier League gravy train. Players are pretty much guaranteed to be millionaires, if not multi-millionaires regardless of anything they choose to do when they finish playing.

At the start of the Premier League era in the early 1990s, £10,000-a-week was seen as a big salary. It quickly went through the roof and, within 20 years, many players were earning ten times that. By 2015, the biggest stars earned in excess of £200,000-a-week and no-one should expect that crazy level of inflation to slow down any time soon.

Wayne Rooney's last contract at Manchester United was worth nearly £300,000-a-week, Sergio Aguero got close to that when he signed for Manchester City and Zlatan Ibrahimovic received the same when he went to Old Trafford in 2016.

The stories of how footballers demonstrate their wealth are many and varied. Gareth Bale has had three real-life golf holes built in his back garden – one from Augusta, one from Sawgrass and another from Troon. It would be safe to assume that Gareth has got enough money to not have to think about working for the rest of his life.

Zlatan Ibrahimovic of Sweden was one player who commanded a massive weekly wage when he signed for Manchester United. (Shutterstock)

Gareth Bale loves golf so much, he has had holes built in his back garden! (Getty)

The talented Ravel Morrison, but has he lived up to the hype? (Shutterstock)

lifestyle, counting his money even though he's never really made it at a top club. He started at Manchester United and then it didn't really work out for him at West Ham. There were a few glimpses, before he went to QPR and then Lazio followed by several loan signings. But even though he's never been a first team regular, he can still enjoy a millionaire's lifestyle. Will it last? Probably not.

Inducements

The way the agent industry has gone has only added to the influence of money and, perhaps more significantly, the willingness of people to make as much of it as fast as possible.

There are now 1,400 'intermediaries', the word adopted by the FA and FIFA when they deregulated the agent business and effectively opened the door for everyone. They are basically the same as agents before but just with a new name.

These intermediaries are inducing players to change their agents. It involves big money and has become one of the biggest trends in football today. This is not to be confused with the 'old-school bungs' culture that would see a proportion of the value of a transfer deal or a 'backhander' being paid to managers or others as part of the negotiations. Now agents pay big money to sign up players. They pay the player or his family to sign up a player on a two-year representation contract.

This phenomenon is not limited to big money for big-name players either. Run-of-the-mill Premier League footballers and even Championship players are subjected to the same kind of inducements to switch from one agent to another.

Payments of £50,000 are common. So, if a player has dropped his agent for another but then falls on hard times later in life, it's highly unlikely they will

Bale, of course, is a bona-fide, world-class superstar, realising his talent and exploiting it to the full. But even modest players, or ones who seemingly waste their talent, still manage to become very wealthy indeed.

Ravel Morrison has been accused by several managers of wasting his talent, not fulfilling his potential. He may look back in years to come with regret and yet he has still earned big contracts at West Ham and Lazio. Sir Alex Ferguson called him one of the best talents he has ever seen, Sam Allardyce lamented his wasted talent and we have only ever seen glimpses of the talent to match the hype. But, for now, he's just enjoying the

••• WHAT THE AGENT SAID

A football fable

Here is a story that illustrates how switching agents can work against a player. It's a true tale, but is not, by any means, unique. It happened to one player but could be a story of dozens of other deals.

There was a player in the Championship. A couple of years ago during the summer, he made it known he wanted a move to the Premier League. Two Premier League clubs wanted this player, but as the transfer window counted down, they ran out of time and ended up buying other players.

Six weeks later, the player rang his agent and said it was time for him to move on. He was signed to his existing agent for another year. But another agent had got in the player's head, and convinced him that he would get him to the Premier League in the next window. And so the player switched to this other agent.

The player had 18 months left on his contract at his club. Just before Christmas the original agent received a phone call from a rival Championship club saying they would bid for the player in January. The player and the original agent were still on talking terms so they met up. The agent told the player: 'You are on £4,000-a-week for the next 18 months, they want to offer you £12,000-a-week on a three-and-a half-year deal.' They were also offering a signing-on fee.

But that night he turned it down because his new agent had convinced him that he had managed to get him a Premier League move. January passed, and the player stayed at his club, thinking he would still get a move to the Premier League. It never materialised. The following year he signed as a free transfer for the Championship club who tried to buy him 18 months before, but now they were not offering him £12,000-a-week but £8,000.

So three years on the player did get his move, but not the one his new agent had promised him – not to the Premier League and for £4,000 less a week than he could have received if he had listened to the original agent. It cost the player £1.2m. And all because an agent had convinced him that he would get him a deal to play in the Premier League. And the craziest thing of all? The player left the new agent and signed for someone else anyway.

receive any sympathy from that agent they spurned. The football business is a very unforgiving one.

The relationship between agents and players has become less and less of a long-standing partnership. They do not stay and work with each other for long enough for that kind of stability to develop. As a consequence, the personal touch – the friendship, even – is lost. That personal bond whereby the agent will care if a player has money left when he retires has been broken.

Broken allegiance

A lot of players switch agents and change all the time because they are enticed by money, gifts or presents. That works against loyalty and forming bonds. In

Harry Swales (front right), who in 1982 was the England football commercial agent. He's followed by Tony Woodcock and Peter Shilton. (Getty)

any industry, if an employee leaves and changes jobs every year then they will never develop a relationship with their colleagues or bosses.

Agents are similarly transient in how they deal with their players. A recruitment consultant does not really have a relationship with their clients because they all move on. That's the hard truth, and it's little different in football.

In many instances, an agent has a player for the summer. That agent will try and move the player on, in order to generate a transfer deal and earn a commission. Once the deal is complete and the agent has got his commission, he will then end his relationship with the player.

Perhaps as little as ten years ago, players would remain with agents for their whole careers. Ryan Giggs stayed with his representative Harry Swales for years. Swales is not a 'big name' in the sense of being high profile. But he was with Giggs from the age of 17 and the pair stayed very loyal to each other throughout the Welshman's career. But that is the exception.

Thick-skinned

Much of the wheeler-dealing going on is based on falsehoods, planting ideas and promising all kinds or riches and opportunities that never come off. Agents will get into players' heads, saying they will get them a better move. They do it all the time – even though they haven't got a deal on the table.

Taxing times

Agents will go to great lengths to sign players. There are rumours in the trade of one big agent who is under intense scrutiny from the taxman. The word on the grapevine is that the taxman has raided this agent's office, looking into allegations that the agent wins business by paying players undeclared but substantial sums of money to sign for him. Bribery, in other words.

Double dealing

But that's as nothing compared to what goes on with some managers. Another story relates to a deal a few years ago for a player to go to a Premier League club. Another agent was working for the club and also happened to be the manager's agent at the time.

In those days, an agent's entitlement to a fee for the transfer of his client was corroborated by a letter saying: 'Club Y will pay you X amount.' The player went to the training ground, had a medical and the deal appeared to be proceeding as planned. Then two letters were produced; one for the player's agent and one for the other agent working for both the purchasing club and the manager. But the letter for the player's agent specified only half of what was expected. When the agent questioned this, the manager said: 'Well, you don't think I'd do this job for

WHAT THE AGENT SAID

Business is business

Everyone understands this is how the business works. They all get on with it, and in truth will look to be equally as ruthless. But for the 'guilty' agent not to take the original agent's calls, or to not at least have the courage to explain what happened – that was what was really upsetting.

The deal with the player probably brought in £150,000 for the new agent. That easily paid for the friend's wages that smoothed the deal in the first place. That is the situation as it stands. In the near future the friend will probably be sacked by the agent from his job. The agent will lose the player at the end of the contract, but no matter. Nothing is lost: indeed, the agent will probably make about £100,000 all told.

It's these kind of situations that explain why agents don't befriend other agents, and keep them at arm's length. Promises of friendship, trust, loyalty count for nothing.

It leaves agents being quite lonely individuals, who only live for the job. I try hard not to be like that. I won't let it take over my life. Others are different. The job becomes all-consuming, an unrelenting, 24/7 occupation. One agent owns a Bentley, and has it driven around for him the whole time so he can just stay on the phone, work from the back seat. Nothing – nothing at all – ever gets in the way of him being able to work and earn money.

nothing do you?' He pocketed £20,000.

This happened all the time. It would happen over the course of years and cover multiple deals. It was basic fraud – skimming a portion of the fee off the top. This would then be split in a variety of ways, with all kinds of people taking their cut.

With friends like these. . .

In the football business, someone is losing out and someone is getting paid. It's how the industry works. This kind of sharp practice bothers people when they first start out in the industry, regardless of their role. But, after years of working in the industry they give up caring. The first time it happens, someone pockets £100,000 and an agent will think: 'What have you done? This is wrong.' The agent will likely be very angry about it. But nothing now surprises the older agents, the more cynical ones. Nothing will shock them anymore.

There is an agent I know with a huge contacts list and who knows many people.

Yet he says that he has only got three friends in this business; only three people that he trusts. One of them is his best mate, another is someone he's known for a long time, and the other is a person I used to work with. As for the rest? He wouldn't trust them, wouldn't particularly want to mix with them and as a result he keeps himself to himself.

If he got married, his best mate would be his best man and even the other two would only get invites to the reception. That's how it works. Agents can't afford to get too close to too many people.

Ask any agent and they will readily admit that they've fallen out with a lot of people. They probably haven't lost friendships as such because they haven't trusted those people in the first place.

But I know of one agent being betrayed by another who he didn't think would let him down. This agent 'stole' a player from him, and did so by offering a friend of the player a job within his company. He dressed it up as having a proper role in the office, but it was nothing of the sort. He would turn up when he felt like it, living off a wage which was effectively just a sweetener to get the player on board. The agent who was the guilty party in this case did not even return the other agent's calls when was trying to find out what was going on. Instead it was left to the friend who was given a job to ring up the original agent, apologise, and admit what had happened.

Even if he was angry, the aggrieved agent did not let people know because that would have shown a weakness. He was disappointed in the other agent. But he was even more annoyed that the person he used to trust didn't return his calls and at least be honest and say that he did it for the good of his business.

Anti-social media

A lot of agents run their Twitter or Instagram account purely to be able to 'tap up' players. They follow the player, the player follows them. It normally happens with young players because older players don't get involved. On Instagram, Facebook, Twitter, the agent befriends them and then direct messages with all kinds of nonsense – 'I'm your man, come to me, blah, blah. Let me have your dad's number', that sort of stuff.

A lot of youngsters have agents already. A lot of kids get agents from 14 and so on, whether it is legal or not. The better, more responsible, law-abiding and ethical agents don't like it, and don't approve of it, but the use of social media to target

players from an early age is rife.

Most agents, from a moral perspective, would say it is wrong. They wouldn't like it to happen to their own teenage children or relatives. As a practice it's lazy. But we all know it happens.

I know one dad of a young boy, who said: 'If you want to speak to my son, come to me. Whether he's 12, 14 or 16, you come through me. You don't go through Twitter.' Yet all of the agents who have tried to sign the kid have got to him via social media. Their excuse will be to say, 'How else can I get hold of him?' Strictly speaking it's not allowed. Transgressors can be reported to the FA. But the sanctions, if any are enacted, are weak and many agents complain they are now always enforced. You have to gain special dispensation to work with minors and if you are caught contravening the rules and making an illegal approach or working with an under age player then the FA can suspend agents.

The old way of doing it was to speak to the young player himself. Child protection ensures – or should ensure – that doesn't now take place. The odd agent will still walk up to a player at a game, approach him and try to convince the player to sign with him. But increasingly it's done via social media.

Talking telephone numbers

Of course, another option for agents to contact players is by getting telephone numbers. There is a lucrative sideline in providing contact details. Scouts – the talent spotters who clubs use to source and identify potential players – often have numbers for in-demand youngsters and will be paid by agents to pass the details on.

Some agents make their approaches using social media as a last resort when

all else fails. But some agents use it as a matter of course. Most would probably not try to contact players younger than 16. A lot of players will follow the agents and message them themselves. They will send the agent a DM asking him to be their agent. It's a two-way street. But, to be brutally honest, they are generally the poor players. They would not be looking for an agent if they were a good player. If they're messaging agents at the age of 17 or 18, then those agents should be thinking, 'Why haven't you got one already?' It is naïve of an agent not to think that they are probably desperate rather than good. That is the sorry truth.

Agents will receive a lot of messages. They start by saying 'I'm a scholar [i.e. a trainee at a club], hoping for a professional contract and will you be my agent?' The better agents are not interested. They politely say no.

Commodity trades

By relying on social media, some agents sign a player without even seeing them play first. Lazy agents do it all the time. The players have to be watched, otherwise how can the agent possibly know what they are selling? Surely a trader has to know about the commodity he is trading.

The better agents will always watch a player first. But sadly, not many agents are like that. They are willing to take a chance because there's simply not enough business to go round. They are willing to take a chance on a player unseen because, who knows – he could be the next David Beckham.

This is the reality of the football business. It's a far cry from the innocence that comes with starting out and even further away from the excitement that goes with being a young player with dreams of making it in the game.

Manchester City U18s celebrate scoring in the FA Youth Cup. Many of these players will already have succumbed to being approached by an agent or may already have one. (Getty)

DISCOVERY

It's the question every aspiring young footballer and parent asks: how does a player get spotted, in order to make the first steps on the road to becoming a professional? There is not one simple, single answer. There are all kinds of ways that talent is identified and recognised by clubs big and small. But one thing is for certain: if you don't get spotted, scouted and developed, there is virtually no chance of making it in the pro ranks. And that is only the start of being exposed to the harsh realities of the game.

'I've seen this kid; he's the new Ryan Giggs'

If people in the game had a pound for every time they've heard the promise that someone has spotted a legend in the making, they would never have to work for a living.

Football is littered with tall stories of the superstars of tomorrow being 'discovered'. It's usually by gnarled old scouts who travel the country and beyond trying to unearth footballing gems. They watch from the sidelines on muddy parks pitches and cast an experienced eye from under their flat caps, while they puff on roll-up cigarettes. Or people walking their dogs, seeing who they think is a child genius having a kick-about with his mates, will phone their local club to proclaim they've seen the new Lionel Messi. Or, more often it's enthusiastic but misinformed parents who think their little boy is the next big thing in football, when he isn't even the next big thing in the school team.

Local football can be a good source of talent waiting to be untapped. (Shutterstock)

Young footballers are often spotted by scouts, scouring the country.
(Shutterstock)

Reality bites

The truth, sadly, is very different. The hardest part of becoming a professional footballer is getting spotted. That is closely followed by getting the right club, the right opportunity and also the right agent. But unless an aspiring player is spotted, he has no chance. So kids and even some fame-hungry mums and dads will go to great lengths to catch the eye of scouts and agents. In fact, just about anyone who they think can put them on the road to stardom. To even get on that road, however, takes time, hard work, and no little good fortune. And it has to start early in life.

Kids' stuff

The youngest age at which players can begin the journey towards professionalism tends to be the under-8s level. Clubs start taking on players from that age group, which means that on a Sunday morning, local junior football teams will have scouts coming to watch games involving players from the ages of six up to 11.

Officially, these scouts have to be wearing club tracksuits, so everyone knows who they are so that they can approach parents and invite the children to go to their club's training camps in the school holidays.

But any coach or scout who is good at their job will have a very good idea if a player has a chance by the age of six, let

alone seven or eight. Clubs are looking for a number of qualities in a player, including game management, understanding the game, understanding what their job is on the pitch and understanding when to pass, and when not to pass. There is an issue at

that age of size because some boys will be much bigger than everyone else and they overpower other players.

Watching a group of young kids play, it soon becomes clear that everyone on the pitch wants to score goals.

Scouts are looking for something different. They want to see an overall understanding of the game. Has a child got the basic skills? Or will he just go gung-ho and run round like a headless chicken? Can he pass the ball properly? Can he control the ball?

Talent spotters are looking for the same kind of basic skills as they would from a 17-or 18-year-old, but the scouts want to see game knowledge as well as the essential skills to be a footballer. At a very young age group, there is still considerable technique involved. A lot of football at that age is just kick and chase. What makes the young players stand out is an ability to do something different.

Can kids be coached for those kind of qualities? It really is more down to instinct. If a player is told he's a defender then defend – don't try and score goals. Knowing the role as a footballer. That's the basis of it.

What a scout looks for

Eighty-five per cent of players of the age of eight will have dropped out of a club's consideration by the time the child is 10 years old. A brutal cull, but it is the reality. This is not to ignore that fact that there are lads who will develop later. At eight, some will be no good; at 10 they might be *very* good. Clubs employ specialised people and coaches who know what to look for in these age groups and how individuals progress within them.

The bigger clubs like Manchester City and Chelsea have scouts who look at eight-to 10-year-olds. They regularly sign them up while others will start slightly older at ages 10 to 12 and so on. The best scouts and the best clubs know more and more about their designated age group and are always gaining experience in developing that knowledge.

The scouts arrive on a Sunday knowing what to look for and respond to a brief. They will look at eight-year-olds, adhering to set criteria according to what their employers want. Every club will be minutely different. Can a player strike a pass? Score a goal? It's very basic at that age. The ones who have got the fundamentals right stand out like a sore thumb.

It is obvious to any observer to notice a little kid if he can control the ball, pass it, strike it correctly, know when to pass and when not to pass; when to go into the space, when to stay and hold position, and show how he can read the game. The boys who have this skillset are conspicuous because there are so many lads who don't have it.

example; Chelsea have one nearby. Many use private schools, such as Manchester City. Another good example is Crystal Palace. The club has proudly boasted a partnership with Hayes School in Bromley to help to get their teenagers to take BTEC qualifications and up to A Levels. Mick Shea, the club's Head of Education and Welfare, said: 'The link we have created with Hayes School will give our players the opportunity to strive for excellence both on and off the pitch.'

Steve Kember has been a key figure at Palace. He has been part of the fabric at the club for decades. He grew up round the corner from Selhurst Park, was a hugely popular player, skipper and manager, and is now chief scout. He was also a PE teacher at Palace's school from where he and fellow staff fed the kids through to the club. That relationship persists. If a young prospect is doing well at the age of 12, he is sent to the school. All his fees are paid by Palace. That represents significant outlay and commitment. The coaching and recruitment team at Palace have to be sure because it's a lot of money that they are committing the club to. Palace chairman Steve Parish even boasted the academy is 'essential' to the club and added: 'For one thing, it helps us establish real deep roots in the community in which we play.'

The kids that have what it takes can be easily noticed by the eagle-eyed observation of a club scout.
(Shutterstock)

In the club

So, a boy has made it, and been taken on by a club. Except he hasn't made it. By any means. This is just the start. He is making his first tentative steps towards becoming a professional footballer in a professional environment. What can a young player and his parents expect?

Education, education, education

All the big clubs have amazing facilities for football. But it doesn't end there. Increasingly, clubs are looking to produce well-rounded individuals as well as top footballers. Many send the youngsters to private schools. That costs a lot of money. But it's all part of the investment. Some clubs have schools on site. Fulham do, for

Early stages

It's probably at 14 when youth footballers reach the key age. At eight years old, a club is taking a punt. A player can be signed to a club for two years then, but most don't sign contracts; instead they get invited to the club to train two or three times a week. It's a process of assessment and progression.

Some youngsters train at two or three different clubs. It's not uncommon for a youngster to train at Chelsea, Fulham

and Palace at the same time, because most players don't sign anything. They get invited in and the clubs have a look at them. Both player and club are keeping their options open.

The sessions then tend to last an hour, doing drills, skill work and then five-a-side matches. It's in these situations when coaches will notice outstanding talent. The moment will come when collectively they decide 'we've got to get him signed up'.

All coaches at all clubs are looking for that unique or exceptional talent. There are definitely special boys out there, the ones who really stand out. To give some real examples, even at eight years of age, it was widely thought that Wayne Rooney would make it. Everton could see it at that age. Jack Wilshere was another – very young, but very talented.

But it would have to be a really special talent at eight or nine for it to be obvious he is going to make it. They would have to be ridiculously special. So at eight years of age, a lot of the training revolves around practice and five-a-sides, with the goalkeepers changing every game. The drills are broken down into sessions of 15

minutes and two games, equating to four lots of 15 minutes in total – an hour.

At that tender age the kids are very impressionable and like to emulate the superstars. There is the odd one who loves a tackle. This will be watched and taken note of. But generally most of the kids just want to score goals.

They will watch Ronaldo celebrate and if he has done a new celebration then they will copy it. Wayne Rooney did his boxing celebration with the two little punches a couple of seasons ago and the next week kids up and down the country were celebrating the same way, doing punches and then falling backwards!

That's when football is at its best for children. Sadly, it's when kids get into the clubs that it becomes toxic for them – because that's when people like me get on their case.

Value

We have seen how major clubs have vast scouting networks. The rationale is to, or at least try to, monopolise talent. It is not that every player will make it – almost the opposite is true. But clubs are desperate

WHAT THE AGENT SAID

Money talks

Just as there are hundreds of tales and rumours about young players being spotted, there are just as many about what kind of financial inducements clubs might make to get talent to come to them. Everybody's heard the stories of clubs giving families a lot of money to sign at eight years of age, or even younger. Many of the top Premier League clubs do it when they know there's a hot property out there. They will often give out £1,000 each time.

Young players are usually signed in two-year cycles: eight to 10, 10 to 12, and 12 to 14. At 14 they can either carry on training with the club until the age of 16 and then be put on a scholarship deal, or at 14 they can be offered what's called an early scholarship, the earliest age at which a player can be offered such a deal. All sorts of promises are likely to be made. The best could easily be promised £10,000-a-week when they sign their first professional deal. But the figures vary greatly.

If a boy is good enough at 14, a club can say: 'We're going to give you a four-year deal now.' This will break down into two parts: two years until he is 16 then a two-year scholarship.

But that's not all. If a boy is at a club at 14 and that club thinks another club will come in to try and poach the player, they can offer a five-year deal with a 'professional' clause inserted to tempt the player to stay – meaning the player can sign a pro deal at 17. This means the club could offer a one-or two-year scholarship. It provides insurance for the club: if another club tempts the player to join them, the original club is due compensation. This is all worked out according to EPPP (Elite Player Performance Plan) regulations to determine if there is any compensation liable. Compensation calculations start from when a player is signed to a club.

So that covers the club's interests. But what about the player's? Clubs will offer families cars, houses, jobs, money, whatever it takes. They will offer long contracts. They will come in for a player at 12 and tell him and his family: 'You are signed until 18.' But to sweeten the deal they might house the family, help them relocate with jobs – basically transform the lives not just of the player but his close relatives as well.

A family from a tough council estate can suddenly end up in a £2m house. They could be coming from some of the grittier parts of Manchester or Liverpool; perhaps live in the middle of Moss Side, then suddenly find they're living in an amazing dream home. At 14 a player can move away from an area, as long as they are still in schooling.

So, even the smaller clubs are giving families £1,000 for eight-year-olds, It sounds staggering but it's only just the start. And all to stop other, bigger clubs from taking the player.

to sign up youngsters because they believe one will come through. That makes the investment and effort worthwhile.

But for the players themselves there's an important distinction. The theory goes that unless a player is top drawer, they shouldn't go to a top club. They can easily get lost in the system, churned up and spat out. If you are an elite player then you have to go to a big club. I think it makes a better player. But the advice would be if you are not an elite player, stay put and assess where you are at 16.

As soon as a player signs a pre-scholarship agreement – which can be

Training is an important aspect of the overall talent assessment.
(Shutterstock)

done at 14 – then he becomes effectively a transfer fee. If the agreement is offered, the player signs on the dotted line. This isn't a scholarship contract, but just the *agreement* to become a scholar. And as soon as that's agreed and signed, then that's it: he is a transfer fee. Then the clubs can ask for what they want, and get any price they want. Then the individual person becomes a commodity. And that's when agents really enter the story.

Special agents

'Agent' has become a bit of a dirty word in football. Some of them are very unpopular with many people in and out of the game. But they are a fact of footballing life and play a massively important part in how the sport, and particularly the business of sport, functions. There are good agents, and bad agents, but like them or loathe them, agents are integral to the modern footballing world.

They are fundamental to how youth football works, as well. The youngest age

an agent will probably go for a player is 12. At 12, that's when players' names begin to be heard more widely in the industry. Partly this is down to technology. There are so many platforms for players to be promoted on now, and to make people take notice. There are show reels on YouTube. There's also a special dedicated platform called FFD.TV. They post video clips of the best young players and all of their latest skills and tricks. It has a cult following as a website and on Twitter. All of the top youngsters are on there.

Among the players on show is an eight-year-old from Chelsea. It features youngsters with outrageous skills and talent. These kind of things grab people's attention and get players noticed.

Fill your boots
But with that attention come other aspects. It's around now that the boys want boot deals. Let's think of a hypothetical example – a really special kid. Let's say he's 'our' kid, meaning he's signed some form of agreement or contract

with a club I work for. He's 12 and he's already got a good boot deal with a major supplier. But there are bigger rewards and incentives on offer.

Two agencies have direct messaged the player on Instagram. A player – an international playing in the Premier League – has done it and another agent has done it. One of them has said to the boy: 'I know your Dad is talking to agents.' Surely that is a disgrace and the Football Association must do something? But what can they do? Well, they choose to do nothing. There are strict rules on illegal approaches. Agents can be suspended and players warned. But, despite the father reporting it, nothing was done.

So the agents have a virtual free hand to target the player. This kid is unique. There's no kid in the country, in Europe, who is like him. Every big club in the country is after him. Every agent worth their salt is after him. There can be really rare occurrences when incredible talents emerge. Agents who have been in their business for 13 or 14 years will suddenly say they have never come across anything like this new boy before. And they'll all want him.

So they have to make the player want to sign for them. We're not talking a nice pair of boots here. They will offer huge packages. Remember the stories of clubs putting up families in houses? Agents will be doing that too. They will help families relocate, find schools, arrange it so the family can rent out their existing home – and that can be a lot of money each month.

The clubs, meanwhile, will give scouting jobs to dads. Whether it's the club or the agent putting money and deals up front, it's a calculated and worthwhile risk because, ultimately, it's a small investment if the kid makes it. Because that one player could be worth £100m in a couple of years.

The boot companies 'are as extensive as the clubs' scouting networks. That is hard to believe, but they really do. Bryan Robson's son Ben is an executive having worked for New Balance. Ben is the son of a British footballing legend and that connection counts. Many of the boot companies use 'football-related' people to establish a link which can make all the difference.

The boot deals are as hot as the football. Nike and adidas have extensive networks. The boot companies and their scouts travel the world. They go to Europe, or wherever they need to. All the boot companies will be present at the

Most of the England players, at all levels, will be affiliated with a boot brand. (Shutterstock)

The all-important boot deal is a good indicator of how a player is perceived. (Shutterstock)

tournaments. Everyone at the 16s level for England will be signed up to some kind of boot deal.

Naturally, every agent wants to be mates with the boot companies. It's a big thing. The football boots cost a lot of money and every player from 14 to 18 wants a boot deal. Families can't afford them, agents don't want to pay for them, and if you've got a connection to get a boot deal then that's a big advantage. The boot companies have scouts. But they usually only look at strikers – sadly, no-one wants defenders!

There are so many examples of players walking out of training grounds and agents going up to them, opening up their car boot and saying: 'Do you want a pair of boots?' And they've got dozens of boots in the car. 'Yup, there you go, sign here – there's your contract.' I know of one player who was approached in this way. He went back and told the club the next day. The agent got banned from the club, the club reported it to the FA but it was not taken further.

Boots are a massive thing to kids. The first thing a 15-year-old will ask is, 'Can

Parents need to be on their guard regarding the unscrupulous tapping-up of players.
(Shutterstock)

you get me a boot deal?' Or: 'Can you get me boots?' It's the first thing they ask every time.

Cashing in

It's just as tough for the FA to clamp down on top clubs signing the best youngsters. One top club have said they would pay £200,000 to get a kid to come to them. Of course it's tempting, but if the player doesn't want to go, he doesn't want to go. But that's how highly the clubs rate these young players. That is an average deal in the Premier League. But we're talking about 11-and 12-year-olds here. It's that much money for such young players.

Agents have even negotiated that kind of figure for young players between clubs in the Championship before. Obviously, the deal is spread over three or four years, the length of the contract. If it was a one-off payment most agents would be retired by now.

I've known players get £2,000 allowances to go into shops every couple of months to get what they want. The best ones, the really good players get formal

contracts, and cash. The best are earning huge sums of money for their age. They will also get bonuses, so if a player gets an England call-up, for example, he will receive a bonus of £5,000.

Tapping up

'Tapping up' is a phrase that has entered the wider football vocabulary. It basically means making an illegal approach to sign a player that does not conform to the rules and regulations. Basically, as the phrase suggests, it means going in through the back door to sign up a player.

When clubs make an agreement for a player, they are committing to making a substantial payment. There is a lot at stake, so everyone involved will do everything they can to make it a success. That means bending the rules – sometimes breaking them. So a lot of the clubs will try and do their deals 'on the QT' and if necessary operate beyond the regulations.

The scenario can work like this. A club wants a player already contracted to another club. The 'buying' club will get hold of the player's dad and invite him in. They are not supposed to – but how does anyone know what people do 24/7? The dad can use any excuse to avoid meeting or communicating with people for the 'existing' club. What he's actually doing is that he's meeting a representative from a Premier League club at their training ground.

All the heads of recruitment tap up parents all the time. They find ways. They will speak to the dads on the side of the pitch. The rules try to stop this. The scouts have to wear club tracksuits. At academy football, all scouts and agents should be in their own area so they can't mingle with the parents on the side of the pitch. But agents and clubs can work around that.

At a younger age-group level, they just make contact how they want. They do tap players up.

Clubs who are fending off interest in their player try and police it, to stop approaches being made, but it's very difficult. Someone from another club who is targeting a player can turn up for a match on a Friday or a Saturday, and say: 'My cousin is playing.' How does the 'existing' club know?' Of course they don't: the person on the gate who lets people in can't know otherwise. So the 'tappers' get around it that way.

It's not just clubs and agents who are at it. Football is a multi-billion-pound industry now. The domestic Premier League TV deal is worth over £5 billion alone and the rewards are so huge for players, for their families and for everyone. That's also why big companies are keen to sign up kids from 11 or 12. Often boot companies go direct to the families, offering 'kit drops'

The Premier League TV coverage is worth bilions. This is a big deal for the clubs and players.
(Shutterstock)

Kieran Gibbs made his way through the Arsenal system. (Shutterstock)

– trips to Nike Town or adidas, where the players will be provided with an allowance and they can get as much kit and leisure wear as they want for themselves or their families.

'Get me a club'

It's all about progressing, getting signed up, developing talent and reaching that crucial age of 14. That's the age when you get offered a scholarship, and you can move away from your home town. It is the point when a player can be offered professional terms, in theory, for years to come.

It is a crucial stage. While the scouting goes on below that, 14 is when people pretty much know: 'This boy has got a good chance' – or 'This boy has got no chance.' Before that age, it is basically a guessing game. That's why clubs have specialists, who know what to look out for at specific age groups.

The players who don't quite make the grade at 14 become desperate. Agents will be inundated with messages from 15-and

16-year-olds on social media. 'Can you help me? Can you help me find a club?' Many agents simply never reply. It's too much like hard work. I stay away from it. I get a lot of messages via social media. But, the truth is, the players have been released for a reason. That's the long and short of it.

But once you get offered that scholarship, that's when you become a big property. And why there are young lads that age being tapped up every day of the week.

Targets

Some Championship scouts now set a target of having 50 per cent of the players on their academy roster to come from their own ranks, i.e. players who have come through from the ages of eight onwards. It is a key ambition for clubs big and small: producing your own players. There are two options – paying big buying in talent, or producing your own players. If they're good enough to break through then a club can rocket up the league. And it could save a club fortunes.

There's a massive emphasis on identifying talent. That's something, certainly, that in the last three to five years has changed greatly. The emphasis has moved towards talent identification. Producing players is what clubs want to do.

All we ever hear of now at a wider level is bringing players through for the national team. If they're that good, and they can come through at Chelsea or Manchester City, then chances are they will become England internationals. The pressure on Chelsea, City, Liverpool and Arsenal is to produce their own players. Chelsea will argue that they do – they just don't play for their own team. But the real end game is getting them in the first team.

Foreign rights

One of the biggest complaints in football today is about the lack of British talent. The accusation against clubs is that they rely on buying foreign players and don't develop British, home-grown talent enough. It doesn't sit right with a lot of people that top clubs in England, for example, field teams without any English players.

That is slightly misleading and unfair. All clubs would prefer to develop their talent 'in house' – that's the goal, because it makes economic sense to develop home-grown players rather than pay a premium to sign players from other clubs.

Arsenal have improved in this regard because they've brought Jack Wilshere and Kieran Gibbs through the ranks. Theo Walcott was a player they signed from Southampton, but he came in at 16. Wojciech Szczesny and Hector Bellerin, even though they are not English, did come through the system. Manchester United have always brought kids through.

Admittedly, Manchester City have little record recently and Chelsea have done nothing. Josh McEachran was supposed to be fantastic, the next big thing, and yet he has faded away. Ruben Loftus-Cheek has played a bit, but not enough. Liverpool have done OK, while more recently Tottenham's youth policy has been bearing fruit.

The ferociousness of tapping up is incredible. So nothing will suit clubs better than to bring through their own players. But the first question for any family before their child signs is: 'Where's the pathway? How do we get into the team?'

Pathways

Chelsea will argue that they help produce players, coach players and bring them through even if it's not for Chelsea. It's a fair argument. Manchester City have no particular record of doing it, at least in recent times. Manchester United can meet with parents and kids and say: 'Look at our record.'

For players and parents, it shouldn't be about the money, it should be about the pathway. Their question should be, 'By coming to your football club, can I make it?' Forget the pay day, and how much he might earn in the future – are they going

Tottenham have had success with their youth policy at the club. (Getty)

⚬⚬⚬ WHAT THE AGENT SAID

Stats and facts

Just like football, even being an agent has gone down the analysis route. A lot of people in football now aren't ex-footballers like they used to be.

It used to be that, with experience from being a former player, scout or coach, you would have an eye for a player. Be able to spot their talent and identify kids who will make it.

But now there has been a move away from traditional scouting. That has been highlighted by the FA abandoning the Talent ID scheme which was credited with putting Dele Alli on the road towards the England team. They would spot players throughout the leagues, identify them at a young age, get them into the FA system, get them into St George's Park and make sure they do not sign up for another country if they have dual nationality.

But now even the FA are moving towards new methods, embracing statistics as to how a player performs rather than trusting the naked eye.

And that's not just the FA either. Even some agents rely on statistics to identify young players for the future.

It's all changed. Football has changed. It doesn't happen like it used to.

and some will do almost anything to get their hands on it. It's always been an ultra-competitive industry, but now there are lots of 'street agents' about who resemble gangsters. Hoodlums.

For the kids who want to make it in the game, they are pushed and pulled this way and that, and can find themselves caught in the middle. Unsurprisingly, many will opt to stick with the kind of people they know, from their own backgrounds and the areas they were brought up in. Some of these people are good people – some are not.

There's one big agent on the scene, a young guy, who is always smart. He comes from a tough background. But he's always clean-shaven, well dressed, always tidy and presentable. He's got a presence, he conducts himself well and he is a great example of how to behave and work.

Others don't really look the part. There's a whole gang of street agents, right across London and the south east, and they've got players of a young age but it can almost be guaranteed that they've got no-one over 19. That's quite rife.

Every agent now has runners, people going to games, watching games, tapping up players. It's such a common thing now that we call them runners because they are running around, trying to sign up players.

Ten years ago, an agent could have their pick and sign any player between 16 and 18. But now there are so many agents chasing players, because there's big money to be made. It's become a very crowded market.

Preferential treatment

Given the number of players, the number of agents, the parents, the clubs and all the competing interests, it has made it very difficult for managers to keep up with everything.

to educate him until he's 16? Is he going to get the coaching, the best facilities and, if he's good enough, will he get near the first team?

Arguably, Man City and Chelsea are struggling because they will always buy the best players. Chelsea do have an argument that they produce kids. But the biggest question is the pathway.

That's why so many kids stay at smaller clubs, because they believe they can get into the first team. But selling the dream is also a big part of it, which is where agents come in again.

Turf wars

Football is a lucrative but cut-throat business. There are a lot of people competing for the potential riches on offer

Many wisely try to stay out of it. There are not many managers that I've ever come across who get that involved. If I rang up a manager and said to him: 'I'm trying to sign this young kid called John Smith, can you put in a good word for me?', some of them would offer to do so. They might do that for two or three agents they get on well with.

A lot of clubs have preferred agents so when kids are in the academy set-up, they will recommend agents to the players; they will say 'that Fred Bloggs is a good agent, we work well with him'. But if you make a specific request to sign an individual player, the attitude might change. Suddenly they might turn round and say: 'Not sure about that, we recommend you go and speak with these ones.'

It's clever. They don't recommend you sign with one, but they tell you to go and speak to three or four. If you are a parent or player and say that you want to sign with someone else who is not on the club's preferred list then they won't explicitly say you can't – they just put on a funny face and tell you to go and speak to their 'chosen' three or four agents first before signing with someone else. They will try and influence it that way.

There have been scenarios where managers have tapped players up for their own agents – i.e., the agents that represent the managers themselves – but it's not as rife as it was 15 or 20 years ago when there were far fewer agents. Back then, it was much more of an 'old boys' act.

Most managers now don't really care. Managers will say that they hate certain agents. But if that agent has got the player, the commodity the manager wants, then you can guarantee he will deal with the agent.

Recommendations

If an academy director says to a young player to sign with a particular agent it will have a bearing on the decision the player makes, but that applies more to younger players, and younger families. Clubs arrange open evenings for scholars and their families, attended by academy directors and various representatives from the club. They or even someone from the board of directors will speak to the player and relatives. Sometimes they will recommend agents to the player and family.

The general outlook from clubs is: 'We don't like agents, but we know you have to deal with them, we know you'll get an agent – and here's a preferred list.' That will have an effect. The family might think they want to give their child the best chance possible, so meet with a preferred agent. If they do that, then the majority of families or players will decide to sign with one from that list of four or five that the club give tacit approval for. But there will

The likes of Chelsea and Manchester City produce home-grown players, but it's fair to say that they purchase the best players too. (Shutterstock)

03

⟨•••⟩ WHAT THE AGENT SAID

Incentives

Deals are always going to happen, but not like they used to. Do agents make pay-offs, or what can be construed as bribes? Of course they do. They can go to clubs and say 'get that player to sign with me and I'll sort you out'. It happens all the time. But it's a different world now. To be fair to the FA, they have clamped down. The press coverage is more intense and if it was happening frequently then it would get out.

If one agent was taking players off another agent, or a manager was putting players onto his agent, then it would get out. There are a few with this nudge-nudge, wink-wink reputation. Nowadays they are given a wide berth.

What is more rife now is the agents offering money to the players. Or incentives back to the players. That's definitely more common now. In terms of the life cycle of a player, most will have come through the club, got a scholarship, been offered a three-year pro deal, broken into the first team and all of a sudden he'll have 300 agents chasing him.

That's when players are offered big incentives by the agents. They are offered percentages of agents' fees, cars, holidays and all sorts of things. That's far more prevalent now. That happens far more now than these old stories of backhanders and bungs, with managers or agents on the take.

If a player is 16, and a big club has come in for him, the floodgates will open to agents tapping up. Phone call after phone call. Social media approaches? That's tapping up. Direct messages? Tapping up.

The players are the ones being offered the backhanders, the incentives and the payments. There are not many old school managers left. In truth there are far more agents willing to pay backhanders than there are managers willing to receive them these days.

be the mavericks who insist on wanting someone else or someone they know.

Why do clubs do it? Because they find it easier to work with agents. They've got relationships with them. The board will have a relationship with these agents and it's simple. They just want to work with them. I don't think there's anything untoward, particularly.

For example, let's say there's a big club which is chasing a youngster. He gets on well with the club, and finds it easy to work with them. A club will want an agent involved to facilitate the signing. No-one gets paid in terms of greasing the wheels and there are no backhanders. The agent just gets paid if the deal happens.

There are probably too many agents now. Back in the day, it used to be an old pals' act and I think it's moved on from there. It used to be very murky – sorting out agents, looking after them, backhanders for the agents and the managers. We've all seen the books about that, the media investigations, and the *Panorama* programme that supposedly 'lifted the lid' on corruption in football. But the reality is such big headlines and allegations have invariably been unproven.

Past and current practice

That said, it was much easier back in the day. You used to get paid an agent fee listed on the back of a single-page letter which said: 'We'll pay you this much on this date.' Now there are about 500 pieces of paper. It's all got to be signed, all above board and you end up signing your life away. It also all goes through the FA's clearing house. It's a different world.

Every agent has an office line to the FA. A number they can call at the FA which has dedicated phone lines, manned by full-time members of staff who work in the department. Most agents have not had any problems with the FA, and they've always been alright with me. They don't care who is being paid. They are just doing their jobs.

They are checking up on deals, going through the paperwork and when things go wrong they go after the clubs rather than the players or the agents.

For all their supposed unpopularity everyone has a preferred agent. Journalists have preferred agents. People that are liked better, who get on well with other people, and have a chat. It's all down to personal relationships.

Of course there is money on offer from clubs to sign players – but nothing really untoward. It's more for the family. If a young player signs for a big club then it can be life-changing money. It's bigger for the player and the family than the agent. Really nowadays, most clubs, 'new-school' clubs, and managers, are not recommending agents for their own gain. It's just because they've got a good relationship with them. It doesn't really happen to any extent now whereby a player is with an agent because a manager told them to and because he is earning something from the relationship in financial terms.

It's more a case of just being down to personal relationships. If you worked in football and your next door neighbour's son was a promising player, the parent would knock on your door and say: 'Our son is 14, he's been offered a scholarship and a pro deal with a club; you've worked in football all your life – can you recommend an agent?' The likelihood is that you would recommend one of the agents you knew.

You'd do it because you like them, want to help and I don't think you would ask for money out of it. My point is that you would recommend someone you trust. Maybe

I'm blinkered but I think it's gone beyond the old school managers who would say: 'Go with him, you must sign with him.' Then the manager, back in the day, would ask the agent for a cut. Those days have largely gone now.

But there are exceptions. One high-profile manager who did sit a player down in front of his agent said: 'Go with him – or you won't get a contract. Simple as that.'

Player power

To get the player to sign with them, agents will offer big money. That's due to the potential financial gain, but with the number of agents there are, it makes business sense, because there is not enough business to go round.

In English football there are 92 league clubs, each of which has on average 25 players. So that's just under 2,500 players in the game. At last count, there were around 1,600 intermediaries registered with the FA. That equates to a ratio of not even two players an agent. That means there's not enough business. It makes sense for agents to target young players emerging in the game and to get them signed up early. So the business now for an agent is to take the money with one hand and give it out with the other.

It's important to realise that by the time most players get to 14, they have never had an agent. At 16, they will have had

Clubs would rather work with agents to make a deal happen. (Shutterstock)

Please sign here. A watertight contract negotiated by a good agent is always a blessing. (Shutterstock)

a couple of approaches from agents, clubs have been interested, a contract is signed and, all of a sudden, agents will be all over them.

There's one kid I know who is barely a teenager. He's a bright prospect, yet he's had 25 or 30 agents, all over him. Already. Phone calls, direct messages – anything to get to him.

That's why the money changes hands between players and agents much more than it did 20 years ago. Back then, there were not so many agents, so there was more money swilling about, more to go round. But it is a tougher market today.

There have been whispers of all sorts of payments going to players to get them to sign with an agent: £50,000 as a one-off; offering jobs to members of the family. That's £25,000 or £30,000 a year. Sharing half an agent's fee is a common one. If the agent earns £500,000 then it could be £250,000 going to the player. At that sort of level agents will offer a luxury car like a Range Rover worth £70,000 and more. It's a lot of money.

Staying the course with agents

The young player nowadays has a difficult decision to work out which way to go. They field so many phone calls from agents. Agents are calling players every day, trying to tap them up. It's probably quite difficult for players. Even as a youngster and certainly as they get older, they always get calls. That's why agents offer incentives and nine times out of 10 the player just takes it.

As a footballer or as a family, if you get 20 different people ringing you, trying to persuade you to sign, then if one is offering £50,000 it's highly likely you're going to say: 'I'll just sign with him, then. He's offering me good money.' They won't really make a decision based on what the agent is like as a person because they view all of them the same, as scumbags.

That's a genuine reason why some players end up with agents and stay with them. There are very few players who will be 100 per cent happy with their agent. But most players can't be bothered to change. Too much hassle. It means they have to do something when they get home from training, and that's too much like hard work.

All that said, there are very few players nowadays who will sign with an agent at 16 and still have the same agent at 36. Ryan Giggs has done. Scott Parker has stayed loyal. Most players will change agents at some point during their career. A player will get an agent at 14 to 17, then when they make it, the big-hitters will offer big money, incentives and all sorts of other stuff and the player will leave his original agent to go with the new one who is offering more money.

It's also self-perpetuating. If one player signs with an agent others will follow suit. A lot is done by word of mouth, and recommendation. A player will say 'My mate is good, go with him.' There's a lot of tapping up between players, as well. One player will go to another, get him to sign for a club, or an agent. If there's an incentive for the player recruiting a colleague, then that encourages such behaviour.

Some agents play the 'street' card to ingratiate themselves with a young player, but the Rolex watch and the Armani bag show they are part of an elite. It's supposed to say: 'Look at me, I'm you, but I've made it, I've got the Range Rover, designer gear and you can be like me.' And it's also a very obvious reminder of the riches in football if a player had made it.

Money and cars on offer can sway a player to a particular agent.
(Shutterstock)

▍ 💬 WHAT THE AGENT SAID

Elite performers

Youth football now comes under the auspices of the Elite Player Performance Plan. The idea is that by the age of 16 every player is with a top club with the principle being that they get the best training, the best coaching and best facilities at the top clubs in a Category 1 Academy to give the kids the best chance of succeeding.

The EPPP youth development scheme was initiated and set up by the Premier League with the idea of improving and nurturing the quality of home-grown youngsters. There are three levels: Categories 1, 2, and 3, and it is also designed to have a fixed system to compensate smaller clubs when players move to bigger clubs.

Sadly, the smaller clubs know they will lose players. That's why we have the unique situation of the player who is at a smaller club. Everyone is champing at the bit, trying to get hold of him because there are not many such players in the system.

Smaller clubs will be resigned to losing him – they know he's gone at some point. Bigger clubs will offer more than what the compensation actually is. They will say: 'We know you are only due £50,000 but we'll give you £100,000 to give us first option.'

Then it's down to the clubs if they want to do that. All the big clubs have been onto the dad. They have asked his club whether they can invite the lad in to have a look. It's all about trying to entice them in, to sell the club to the family and to persuade them to sign.

But don't forget the agents in all this. You get some who are trying to sign players from 12. Take that really special kid again who has been with an English club, outside of the Premier League, and he's not yet signed up by one of the big clubs. The clubs are all over him. And the agents are all over his dad.

His father is in a unique position because his son is the only 12-year-old in Europe who is that good and not at a top club. That's the unique nature of it. There's no other special 12-year-old – and we are talking very special – who is not signed to Chelsea, Manchester City, Barcelona or whoever. That's what makes this kid special and unique.

If ever you wanted an example of spotting, developing and polishing a youngster into becoming a top professional footballer then this kid is the best.

And that's why every club, agent and scout has been after him and his dad for a long time. We are talking about an elite standard player here.

Chelsea will try and sign players like him and they will make the point to the parents that being around better players will make him a better player. It's not necessarily just about the coaching. Chelsea can't guarantee first team football, but being around better players, playing with a better standard of players and, while, by the time he is 18, training with top players will make him improve – but if he stays at his existing club then he won't be as good. That's Chelsea's argument.

The idea, at the end of the day, of EPPP is to ensure the best kids are in Category 1 academies because they believe that's where they'll get the best coaching, play with the best players and improve that way. Not everyone is convinced it works, but whether you agree or not, that's the theory. Being around and playing with the best, according to the theory, makes you improve.

SCRAMBLE

So, the question is: how is a child turned into a professional footballer? Or, is it really possible to mould a five-year-old into a Premier League superstar earning millions, winning trophies and fulfilling every schoolboy's dreams? There must be a starting point and, in most cases, the best players have football in their genes. That connection to the game is invariably in their blood. If their dads weren't professional footballers, they were huge fans who took their sons to games as soon as they could walk, bought them a ball and got them playing as quickly as possible.

The next big thing

'The next big thing' is the prospect every club is after. He has got every attribute needed. That is why every big club in the country is after him.

Skill, enthusiasm, pace, touch and the right mentality. Put that together and the best kids will make it to the very top and come through the crowd. That's why all the big clubs are ready to throw huge money at the best children or, initially at least, at his parents.

There is, right now, or at any given time, one kid who stands out from the crowd.

He is the most sought-after kid of his generation. This happens on a very regular basis. It comes in cycles. There is one child, the talk of youth football, the talk of Premier League scouts, the talk of agents. They all know how good he is and they want a piece of the action.

Red hot

To illustrate this, we are going to look at a typical case of an emerging youngster. We could be talking about one today, next year, the year after that or the best kid in five years' time.

The stakes can be high for a child that shows promise – is he the next big thing? (Shutterstock)

Wayne Rooney in FA Cup action for Manchester United vs Arsenal. (Getty)

But if we're talking about how to become a professional footballer then our young superstar in the making needs some help and some guidance to fulfil his incredible potential and reach the top.

Most talented kids will have football in their upbringing and usually in the family. His dad might have played semi-pro. His dad will know how good he is. He will know that from watching his son but he will also know because his phone is red-hot. Everyone knows his son is a talent in demand and they all want him.

Every agent, every big club and every scout is trying to badger his dad every day of the week. In fact, a few less scrupulous agents will have been contacting the kid as well. You cannot represent kids under 16 but some agents will try anything.

National treasures

They are all looking for the next Wayne Rooney, Steven Gerrard or Dele Alli. And the best kids will go on to play for their countries. The really special ones will be marked down as teenage superstars, breaking into the first team at 16, just like Rooney.

Rooney has received huge criticism throughout his career but as a teenager thoughts about an unknown future didn't matter. When he was at Everton in the youth team, he was regarded as the best in the country, the best teenage talent. He burst onto the scene. His career has been an incredible success.

Family matters

Rooney was born into a football family. Right now there's one kid coming through who is living in very similar circumstances. He was born into a football family. He's been playing for a smaller club, at under-12s, not in a Premier League academy, and that's why all the big clubs want him. They can snatch him now knowing that if he carries on his progression then he will be a sensation.

There are academies springing up everywhere catering for those young kids

whose dream is to be a pro footballer. And not only academies set up by the clubs, operating as big businesses in their own right looking for talent and prospects. There are also football academies independent of clubs that are specifically designed to spot young talents and recruit them to their ranks.

Talent nurseries

Children will play some form of organised football from the age of five. Usually they start at six or seven playing football on Sundays. Some will play for local teams or the independent academies, some of these set up by ex-pros.

This is a growing area of player development. Parents will be charged £5 or £10 a session for their children to be trained by decent coaches. It's a good 'earner' for the former player, but like everyone else he will be hoping that one of the kids he coaches might be a big talent.

Club scouts see the child players at five or six, and if they are sufficiently impressed,

invite them to come and visit the clubs the scouts represent. Football has tried to change in the wake of the various sex abuse scandals which have come to light in the last few years, centring around youth developments in the 1970s and 80s.

The Football Association has reinforced existing rules – and publicised them as well as setting up new rules to try and ensure such scandals are never repeated in the future.

The FA has set up a hotline for anyone to call and report incidents. Criminal record checks are required in line with legislation and government guidance. The clubs have to ensure that Disclosure and Barring Checks have been made. Anyone aged 16 or over has to undergo these checks before they can work with children or young people.

Clubs also employ welfare officers to help ensure rules and standards are adhered to.

There is a high turnover of young players, so many kids going through

Youth football teams are very popular, often playing on a Sunday or after school.
(Shutterstock)

the system, all desperate to make it. Professional clubs will have hundreds of very young players who make some kind of entry into the system. Most will never make it past the stage of initial interest, but a small number will stand out. Initially this will likely be because of size: their basic, superior physical strength and power over their peers makes them better. But when the others catch up physically then the focus is more on the skill and technique showing through.

The clubs are playing a numbers game: get in as many as they can and then hope one really comes off.

Toddlers

To outsiders, this will understandably sound very cynical, and not without controversy. It can be viewed as exploitative for what are effectively large businesses and globally famous brands using very young children in this way. Kids start kicking a ball in the back garden when they are old enough to run. Some will start even earlier – the stories of a player never being without a ball even before he was a toddler are common. At that stage it is entirely innocent, just a little child enjoying playing with a football simply for the fun of it. The child is obviously not thinking about being a professional footballer.

But from the ages of five upwards, children are dreaming of growing up to become a professional footballer. They copy the celebrations, wear the same boots or wear their socks over their knees. They grow their hair long like Bale. They are trying to copy their heroes.

Role play

The debate over whether footballers are role models or not is long and fiercely debated. There are experts in the field who can point to good, hard evidence that it's not remote, distant superstars who children only see on television who influence and mould their characters and behaviour, but the people children actually interact with on a daily basis – parents, adult relatives, and teachers, for notable examples.

The other view is that children *are* influenced by footballers. I share that opinion. From my experience it's obvious that players have a bearing on how a child behaves. The kids copy their every move from their looks and the way they play, to their behaviour on and off the pitch. They copy goal celebrations, mimic their camera-friendly gestures, and sadly, their less appealing characteristics.

At such a young age, these children are probably – hopefully – not thinking about the money or the glamour. They want to play football, that's their dream. That's all they want to do – play for their favourite team, play for their national side, win the World Cup. It's the familiar stuff of innocent childhood fantasies.

The lure of money probably doesn't raise its head until they are around 16 and it only starts around then for most of the kids because it is visible to them, especially in a club environment where they see the big-name first team players arriving for training in mega-expensive supercars. It's then that they realise that if they make it, they will soon be driving a £250,000 car of their own. Where once they were trying to emulate footballers for the way they played, now it's for what their talent rewards them with. Innocence is swiftly lost.

The special one

So, the clubs have signed as many young players as possible and they are now looking to mine one gem from each year or age group. Do that, and the club and its scouts will have done very well.

Every so often, of course, along comes someone *really* special and they will stand out an absolute mile. Wayne Rooney is the obvious example. Everyone knew he would make it from a very young age, and not just at Everton. Ross Barkley is another.

What also links those two players is that they were boyhood Everton fans. It was clear they had a connection, and an extra hunger and incentive to make it: they wanted to become professional footballers but with *their* club.

Contrast this with Raheem Sterling. Born in Jamaica, he grew up in Wembley and was initially signed to QPR before moving to Liverpool. When he left to join Manchester City, he made it clear he felt leaving Liverpool was the right thing to do for the good of his career, pushing himself

and developing his talent to help him grow as an England player. He had no real connection to Liverpool. They were not 'his' team. As a kid, Sterling supported their arch rivals Manchester United.

Those are the differences between the kid who grows up as a fan and the other kid, the one who has a different mindset.

Ross Barkley (right) in action for England. (Shutterstock)

Influential former England player David Beckham has been a role model on and off the pitch. (Shutterstock)

Both are driven and have a hunger to get to the top. But Rooney and Barkley had a different kind of incentive. Whichever path they follow, they are brilliant players who reached the top. And that's not because they supported one team or another, or had ambition but primarily because they had wonderful natural talent, given to them as a blessing. It can't be said with too much certainty but it must be in their genes.

Roy of the Rovers stuff and nonsense

Of course every kid has dreams of playing for who they support. If they grow up supporting Manchester United, the thought of playing at Old Trafford is overwhelming. Imagine being a 10-year-old prospect at United and having the potential to play at Old Trafford, The Theatre of Dreams.

But this is entering the realms of naivety. If a young player grows up as a Tottenham fan and Chelsea offer him £1m, he will sign for Chelsea. If a diehard Arsenal fan is approached by Spurs and they offer a good contract, then the player signs for Tottenham.

The clichéd Roy of the Rovers stuff, whereby players sign for who they support, play for less money and don't win anything just because of the badge? It doesn't happen. It doesn't exist.

It's hard to believe it ever existed. Jamie Carragher grew up an Evertonian, but

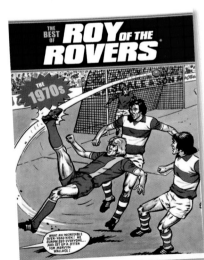

Roy of the Rovers has most likely provided inspiration to a wealth of would-be footballers.

won the Champions League with Liverpool and is now an Anfield legend. Playing for boyhood heroes does still happen but only when the player is amply rewarded for doing so. The days when players would walk to the stadium and mingle with the fans have long gone. That era died along with black-and-white television.

Watched and monitored

There are still assumptions that if a precocious five-year-old who stands out a mile from the rest has been noticed and taken in by a club that a career in football awaits. Even if the child does not make it with that club, he has surely shown enough talent to succeed at some level.

The truth is very different. This is just the start of a very long road which very few will reach. There are so many obstacles and it's not just about talent but also mentality, how these players not only develop as footballers but live their lives and grow up.

'Watch what you eat'

Clubs will watch and monitor the boys from a very young age. They will carry out medical tests later, including heart tests, probably from the age of 16. They will undergo medicals before signing contracts but will also keep checks on kids even before then to make sure they stay on track. The clubs will want to make sure the kids are fit and healthy before they sign them, just as the FA will want to be sure of their well-being before getting them into the England set-up at whatever age.

It goes across various issues. For example, if a 14-year-old gets a little overweight then the club might intervene and say to his parents: 'You'd better watch what he eats.' One talented youngster, now at a Premier League club, was struggling to complete games and had no energy by about the 70th minute let alone 90 minutes. They were able to identify an issue and boosted his energy levels with medication to help his blood and circulation.

This kind of intense management and control happens because if the player is

Ruben Loftus-Cheek reportedly was a very young millionaire.
(Shutterstock)

💬 WHAT THE AGENT SAID

Kids get £1m pay day

It's been reported that Ruben Loftus-Cheek – a brilliant young prospect at Chelsea – got paid £1m. Wayne Rooney's family was offered a lot of money to sign for different agents, to sign for different clubs as a youngster and the rewards are massive.

It will be interesting to see what tomorrow's youngsters – our young hopefuls – get when the time comes. And that's why so many parents – if not the kids themselves – will do anything to reach the top, live life through their children and hopefully reap the huge rewards on offer within football.

That's why it is understandable the sacrifices that parents make, and they are ready to do whatever it takes. Parents and families will change jobs, move house, put their other children into different schools, and uproot the family because the rewards are so great.

They've seen young men earning £250,000-a-week, and will ask themselves, 'Can my son earn that?' For all its transformation in recent years, football is still a working class sport. A lot of players and their families come from council estates and humble backgrounds. All of a sudden they can see pound signs tantalisingly dangling in front of their eyes.

Football can change lives. It has the ability to change a player's life, his family's life and if both are ready to make sacrifices then the rewards are incredible.

Technically, you can only sign a pro contract at 17. But, of course, clubs try to find a way round it to keep their best young talents happy. Youngsters can sign as a scholar from the age of 14 and, when they are the very best of the best, clubs will often make a longer-term

promise. They know they will be signed until they are 17, can then sign a new three-year professional contract and, at 18, can sign for even longer. While some kids are sweating every year from 14 onwards, all the way up to 19 as to whether they will get a proper contract, the best and most sought-after youngsters are on a big money promise. And it's a promise the clubs will always keep – otherwise word quickly gets around

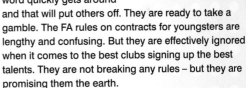

and that will put others off. They are ready to take a gamble. The FA rules on contracts for youngsters are lengthy and confusing. But they are effectively ignored when it comes to the best clubs signing up the best talents. They are not breaking any rules – but they are promising them the earth.

In those contracts there will also be an allowance for the family. There will be a signing-on fee and a family allowance as well. It's completely above board. Clubs can pay whatever and whoever they want in a contract.

That could be £200,000 for the kid, £50,000 for the family. It's completely above board. The money in football has gone crazy. These kids are being paid too much. They don't need to be paid so much. The problem is that if as a club, you don't, someone else will. It's as simple as that.

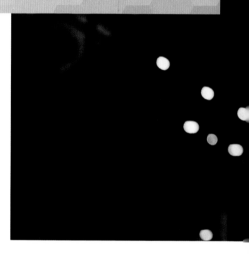

💬 WHAT THE AGENT SAID

Wining and dining

There have been stories circulating in the game of all sorts of things agreed in contracts. The most common is unlimited flights for foreign players. For a London kid signing for a big northern club, they will be offered free travel for the player and the family as well.

These are pretty standard 'extras'. Travel is an almost regulation perk in a deal for players aged 16. From 14, clubs will usually move the family. They can put the child into private school and include all the travel to and from school to the deal.

A product of the Fletcher Moss junior club in Manchester, Marcus Rashford. (Shutterstock)

technically very good then the club will want to ensure every possible effort is made to get the best out of him. At that age it's mostly about watching and monitoring kids. They want to develop them, train them and make sure they get every possible chance of success.

In the professional game, at senior level, it becomes far more intense and closely controlled. Clubs will check diets, monitor every aspect of health and well-being and assume near absolute control. Kids are monitored but not to the same levels as when they get older, when they have to go through tough medicals before signing multi-million-pound playing contracts.

But a lot of parents will not be thinking of anything but their kids making the grade. The rewards are so great. It's life-changing money for the kids and their families. Look at the parents' faces and it's almost possible to see the pound notes clocking up before their very eyes. They will do anything to see their son reach the top.

Perks and privileges

A couple of boys who went from one big club to another got all the travel and hotels paid. Whenever the families go to see them, they get their hotels paid. It's always

a nice hotel, a Marriott or a Hilton. The families get put up, wined and dined.

The car's the star

Families will ask for cars. It will be phrased as a 'car allowance', supplied and paid for by the club. The club always sorts such an arrangement out. To what extent will depend on how much they want the player. But generally the bigger the club, the more expensive the car.

It's hard to think of anything clubs will not do if the young player they are after is that good, and if they think that he is going to make it all the way into the first team. There's almost nothing the club won't do to sign the best kids to get them on board. Unless it is something stupid, they will do it. They'll break the bank, put the parents up in hotels, treat them to meals, flights, etc.

The demand to sign the best young players is immense. It illustrates the pressure and the demands placed upon the recruitment departments and talent spotters employed by clubs. It's why agents work so hard for so little reward.

Sunday morning shockers

The best scouts will be obsessive when it comes to watching Sunday morning football.

The regular places for the scouts to go will be the best areas or teams in London, Manchester or Birmingham and elsewhere which have a deserved reputation for producing good footballers. For example, one London youth team, Senrab, has become famous and synonymous with producing the likes of John Terry, Ledley King and Bobby Zamora. In Manchester, it was the Fletcher Moss junior club which has produced young players like Marcus Rashford, Danny Welbeck and Ravel Morrison. If they have a good tradition, then logic suggests they are doing something right with producing good youngsters and there will be more in the future.

The scouts will know exactly where to go, who to look at and who to speak to. They'll be there every Sunday morning to look at the best kids in the hope one of those municipal pitches will throw up the next superstar.

At the junior level, there are often 20 games going on at once at one location. There are 100 families watching. On one side, the scouts – if they are there – are standing with the coaches.

John Terry (inset) and Ledley King, who came through the ranks at Senrab youth team in London. (Shutterstock & Getty)

Every Sunday morning agents are at under-14s or 15s games. They hear bits and pieces about players and try to be incognito to watch them, look at them, get to know them. They will be looking at the best young players and even observing their families on the touchline. The clubs will want to see what sort of families and backgrounds they come from. Whether they have all the right foundations to make it as a player. Then they will weigh everything up and if there's a deal to be done, if it's a good kid they want to sign then they'll do anything to make it happen and they'll be back week after week to look at the best kids.

That's where the scouts do their business and spot the next superstar. The scouts will know their area. They might be part-time, or even youth coaches themselves, earning a retainer or getting a regular payment from clubs.

They really know their market and often you see the junior scouts progressing and later getting jobs at clubs. Arsenal have a reputation for bringing kids in and those scouts who signed the likes of Tony Adams were given jobs because they clearly know who and what they are looking for. That's the story of Steve Rowley, Arsenal's chief scout. He spotted Adams and a whole raft of other young players and is still on the senior staff. It's the same the world over in football, a process of progression and working your way up.

Rule-breakers

For the agents, it's very different. Under FA rules, they can sign youngsters in their 16th year.

It's a big concern that a lot of these kids aren't allowed – or supposed – to have agents until they are 16. Then clubs are faced with the ridiculous situation of having a player since the age of eight, who they have nurtured and brought through and then suddenly an agent crops up when they turn 16. They come in from nowhere and now the club has something different and challenging to deal with.

The reality is that, despite the rules on being represented only from the age of 16, plenty of agents are already working with kids at 14 because they know by then whether they can get the player a contract with the club. That's when agents get really busy, even if they can't formally sign them until their 16th year.

At 14, a player can sign for a club, on what is termed a scholarship deal, up to the age of 16. They can offer it to the player in writing along with a pre-contract. That's why 14 is the typical age when boot companies, agents and clubs all chase the kids in the talent pool. The interested parties will have a rough, but good idea by then. They will know whether the kid can make it, reach the top and have the potential – and it's all still about potential – to become a Premier League superstar of the future.

There's always the odd exception with players who are younger than that. There are also some instances of individuals at 14 of whom it is not expected they would make it yet at 16 they will show they can. But those are the exceptions.

Teenage kickers

There are always names circulating, whispers doing the rounds, and word on the grapevine about who will make it; who the next big thing is, the next young superstar at Arsenal, Chelsea, Manchester City or wherever.

Reiss Nelson at Arsenal became pretty special and his name was being spoken about from those in the know from about

Tony Adams (second from left) was spotted by an Arsenal scout. He's seen here sandwiched between Ian Wright (left), Ledley King and Les Ferdinand. (Getty)

Reiss Nelson (left) during an Arsenal training session. Nelson was noticed as being a considerable talent at a young age. (Getty)

The unscrupulous football agent – friend or foe?
(Shutterstock)

when he was 14. Dom Solanke, Tammy Abraham, and Loftus-Cheek were all being spoken about at 14. The interest builds from a young age.

There is an England under-15 side and that fuels interest in 14-year-old players, making it the pivotal age for development and increasing interest. Younger than that

💬 WHAT THE AGENT SAID

Teenage tapping-up

The best players at 13 will be getting approached and pressured to enter into agreements with clubs in ways that don't strictly adhere to the rules. In others, they are being 'tapped up'; and at 14 it is happening left, right and centre. It might sound completely unethical but it is happening, and happening now.

There is an amazing story about one of the best kids being tapped up by two agents. In truth, this sort of thing happens on such a frequent basis that it should not surprise anyone. But this particular story was still shocking – because there was clear proof.

A player was being tapped up. There was clear evidence of this in the form of direct messages and texts. Such methods are crude and obvious. Those sending the messages were clearly breaking the rules. Yet there still seems to be a reluctance to do anything about it. Finally, the FA took some action against an agent, who was suspended. But they seemed reluctant to do so judging by the length of time and number of complaints made by the boy's parents before the FA took action.

One of those doing the tapping up was a current first team Premier League player. The messages are all there. Sent via Instagram. 'I've heard you're a great player – can I have your dad's number.' That player was acting on behalf of his own agent.

Another young agent did it for one of the bigger agents. Again, messages were sent; a virtual paper trail was there, making it an open-and-shut case of rule-breaking by agents.

All of the proof was e-mailed to the FA by the parents but nothing was done about it. The FA did sweet FA. The only conclusion to be reached was that they were not interested in it. A problem is they probably have not got the appropriate rules or punishments to fit the crime.

is hard to predict; older and a player has already taken shape and most clubs will have 14-year-olds who are agreed scholars and they will really think have got a chance.

Banned, named, and shamed

The really sad part about that story is that the authorities were allowing a young kid to be tapped up. The agents involved should have been banned, and the Premier League player also.

Good agents will find loopholes that enable them to escape sanction but at the very least they should have been banned or named and shamed. But the FA could not or did not do a thing. Many agents view the FA on things like that with contempt and as being worse than useless. The FA and people in the game look down their noses at agents and yet they do nothing about the agents who break the rules.

Agents will go to great lengths to get hold of the best young players. They will send youngsters shirts, boots or even pay them. But all this does is to encourage families of youngsters to demand money,

generally because other agents have offered to pay them.

Paid to play

If a family is ready to sign for an agent just because he's offering cash it shows they place no value on what a good agent can actually achieve in the long term. I know of an agent who asked a family: 'You would sign with me if I pay you? It would mean I might not be the best person but you'll sign with me just because I'll give you money. How do you know I just won't take that money back?' Because that is what *will* happen.

Families will demand up to £2,000-a-month even for young players. The best response from those of us in the agent industry would be to simply say: 'Thanks very much, I'll walk away, see you later.'

Players have been getting paid a lot by agents recently. But it is delusional to think that agents will not want to recoup that up-front investment. And relationships tend to break down when agents upset players by using the tricks of the trade to get that investment back.

💬 WHAT THE AGENT SAID

Trust the experts

It pays to be noticed – but leave the scouts to do the noticing. Nowadays, boys are running round, going up to the scouts and shouting: 'Come and watch me!' That's what it's like every weekend.

But be warned, success-hungry parents – the clubs can easily be put off by unsolicited claims, especially from the parents. Dads and mums can be overpowering. Too many parents are living their dreams through their kids. 'Imagine me one day sitting there at Stamford Bridge, watching our boy play.'

The magnitude of the potential financial rewards are huge. Everyone wants to jump on the gravy train; everyone wants a piece of the money pie. For most parents it's not really about that calculation. They love to be part of the development of their son as a player, especially the dads. You can see their chests bursting with pride. They can't help themselves from telling people. 'We're off to Cobham with Chelsea tonight for training,' brags the dad to his mate at work. Parents love that.

It's good to have pride, and dreams and ambitions, but making claims for your own child can be counter-productive.

Pushy parents can inspire their kids, but also potentially ruin chances of success.
(Shutterstock)

05

TEENAGE ANGST

The teenage years are so fraught for an aspiring player. It's make or break time – will they join the professional ranks or be cast aside to try and rescue a career somewhere else or leave football altogether? For clubs, it's a time when they like to hedge their bets.

Jamie Vardy is perhaps the best example of how heartbreak doesn't necessarily mean the end for a player if he doesn't make it. If at first you don't succeed, try, try and try again. Vardy was released from Sheffield Wednesday at 16. But at 14, while the coaches and decision makers at Wednesday would not have been sure about whether Vardy would be a success, they would have given him two more years to prove himself.

That's because if coaches are certain on a player, they give them a pre-scholarship contract. If they're not sure they offer a two-year deal and they will wait to see how the player 'trains on' from 14 to 16, during which time they can offer a contract. Once again, it proves that 14 is perhaps the most important age in the development of a player. It is at 14 that a player can be offered a scholarship. That is the first step towards being signed up by a club.

On the scrapheap – at 16

From the January of the player's 14th year, the club can offer what the clubs call a pre-scholarship. They offer it in a letter to the family and, from the moment the family agree and say they will sign it, the player then effectively becomes a tradable asset: a transfer fee. It is a crucial factor in the rationales and decisions a club makes about its youth policy.

'Sorry son'

Let's be clear here: only the minority make it. Ultimately, the majority do not make it. But there is a big group caught in the middle – the ones they are not quite sure about and can go either way. Clubs will have one or two at the top end who are offered a contract and one or two at the bottom end who they have already pretty much made up their mind on.

The majority will be in the 'undecided' category. At 16, Sheffield Wednesday would have eventually said to Jamie Vardy: 'Sorry, son, you're not good enough.' The same goes for Charlie Austin, who was rejected by Reading as a youngster,

Reflecting on that rejection years later, Vardy said he was released because he

◄◄
Against all odds, Jamie Vardy has shown he is a worthy player.
(Shutterstock)

▶
Sometimes being a smaller player has its advantages, as Iniesta from Spain has shown time and again playing for club and country.
(Shutterstock)

was too small. It would be good to think that by 2017 or 2018, football has moved beyond that old-fashioned view. Clubs cannot keep saying: 'You're too small, son.' Not while the game has had Xavi and Iniesta as examples of two of the best midfield players the world has ever seen.

Size matters

To be a centre half or a goalkeeper, a player needs to have height and physical size. Arsène Wenger used to have a rule of thumb that keepers had to be 6ft 3in or 6ft 4in.

Shay Given is a great example of Wenger's preference, because he was linked with Arsenal and was an international, top class keeper. But he was never going to Arsenal. No matter how good he was, Wenger apparently had this thing about 6ft 4in keepers. The only exception you can think of is David Ospina. He's on the shorter side, but even he's listed in some places as being above 6ft.

Tony Pulis also likes bigger keepers. Julian Speroni was in goal for Crystal Palace. But as soon as Pulis became manager at Selhurst Park, he looked to 'bomb' Speroni out. In came Wayne Hennessey.

So some managers are looking for very specific things in players. But at 14 or 16, it's too young to be so specific and exacting.

Pressure and pitfalls

So, whether or not a player makes the grade as a professional often comes down to that crucial period between 14 and 16.

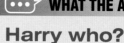 **WHAT THE AGENT SAID**

Harry who?

When Arsène Wenger spoke about his regret at Arsenal letting Harry Kane go to Tottenham when Kane was a kid who had trained with the Gunners, Wenger was talking in general terms about clubs missing out on promising talent that was within their grasp.

There is no way that even Wenger, who has such a comprehensive knowledge on players and youngsters, would have had an input when Kane was 11 and left Arsenal to join Tottenham. First-team managers don't get involved with individuals at that age. They have to trust the youth coaches, academies and scouts. But the managers will probably start to know about players from 14 and upwards.

Basically, from the time the club signs them as potentials at 14, those players have two years to prove themselves worthy of a scholarship at 16. It is a big pressure on them and many will fall by the wayside at 16, their dreams in tatters. Some will simply give up.

Broken dreams

Jamie Vardy was released at 16, while Charlie Austin had to go on a tortuous

route via Poole Town to make it in the game. Vardy went into non-league himself and has come back into international football, breaking Premier League goal-scoring records in the process.

That's a great example of how it is possible for rejected youngsters to come back and it's fantastic to see. It's so sad to witness so many kids aged just 16 who have just been 'bombed'. Understandably they become desperate, and message agents on social media – Twitter or whatever – to plead: 'Can you help me?' They are desperate and it's hard. Their dreams have been broken.

For any kid who gets released – and this is a great shame – at 15 or 16, hardly any will think about going into non-league football. They all want a league club. If you suggest that to them they see it as a mark of their own failure. That's one of the reasons why it's fantastic that Vardy, who was forced to drop down into the non-league system, has set up his own academy to try and bring through youngsters on a similar path to his own.

Route back

The FA and the non-league clubs should be making more of a concerted PR campaign to highlight the positives that can be learnt from the examples of Vardy and Austin. They can point to those players and prove that being released by a Championship or League One club, let alone a Premier League outfit, is not the end of the world. It doesn't mean a teenage player has failed. There is a route back into the professional game. It is worth repeatedly looking at Vardy. Years on from that enormous disappointment of rejection, he made it into the England team. It proves you should never give up. Forget the money side. Vardy is now of course earning huge wages, but his story is more

about coming back, proving himself and making it at the elite level. Now, of course, having been instrumental in Leicester City winning a league title, he is a major star and could command even high wages at bigger clubs.

Making the grade

The best young players are offered pre-scholarships in their 14th year. At lower end Championship or League One and League Two clubs, then coaches will have to push for their clubs to offer pre-scholarships for players that those coaches are sure on. Those clubs are run on a budget; it can be ruthless but if a coach believes in a player then he will have to fight for the player to be signed if not everyone is in agreement. Sometimes it's about them being too small or late developers and clubs are often nervous about taking the short or slight boys on.

Teenage boys of course will grow at different times and develop at different rates, so between the ages of 14 and 16, clubs will need to have some kind of flexibility in their decision making.

The best 14-year-olds will get a scholarship and the promise of a longer deal in the future. That way, it stops the best youngsters slipping away.

Lock and key
The best of the best get promised the earth at 14 – even the promise of a pro contract to make sure they have no thought of leaving.

At 18, players can sign a five-year professional contract. The best youngsters at Premier League clubs will thus be under lock and key. Even the best at Championship clubs or below who do not have the same financial resources will be well looked after, otherwise their clubs

know the top clubs will pounce and steal their precious talent away.

The top boys will get a signing-on fee with their first pro contracts, and get from £1,000-a-week to £10,000-a-week. Some clubs will pay the families a lot of money, draw up contracts for them and make sure they are well looked after.

Fear of failure

It is hard to know who will come through. There have been lads at 14 or 15 who, it seems obvious, have got no chance. Yet by 21 they are in a Premier League first team. The opposite is also true: lads at 14 or 15 who look for all the world that they are going to be big players are suddenly building a wall down a building site at 21 because they just did not develop or fulfil their potential.

Confidence
At 14, the club will have an idea as to whether they think a player will make it or not. But as far as the players go, they all think they're good enough. They all believe they will make it, they will all become top players. Maybe they need that confidence

Jamie Vardy chats to one of his academy graduates. (Getty)

Poole Town was the proving ground for Charlie Austin. (Getty)

Chelsea U18s in jubilant mood after scoring against the Arsenal U18 team. (Getty)

to believe they are going to reach the top. None of them want to ever think about failing. Arrogance would be the wrong word. It's more about being scared of failure. They don't want to ever think about it. They must believe they'll make it.

One-upmanship, teenage style

We've already seen how players are competitive with each other over everything. That phenomenon rears its head early. At 14, players are already engaged in games of one-upmanship. As a result, a lot of football clubs don't like their young kids going off to international duty. In fact, they hate it. Their players can join up with national under-16s sides at 15 and, while no-one will admit this publicly, the kids come back from training with these representative teams as different people. They suddenly become arrogant little so-and-sos.

The whole culture of football is built on one-upmanship, the notion that 'I'm better than you, I've got more than you.' It becomes a case of 'I've got a prettier girlfriend than you, a better house than you, a better car than you, better shoes than you, a better watch than you,' not just 'I'm better at football than you.' A dressing room culture is built on that. And all that starts at a very young age.

And, naturally, players will boast about who represents their interests: 'I've got a better agent than you.'

Golden rules

There is one agent who has got a golden rule that if a kid asks for boots and the agent says he will honour the request, then he gets them to the player within seven days. It's good PR for the agent. Football works on word of mouth to a large extent and that player will speak to his friends, telling them how good his agent is. He might say: 'My mate wants to speak to you – is that alright?' If this friend is a decent player, then the agent will be keen. But if the player is telling the other kid that it took him a month to receive a pair of boots from the agent then the opportunity to forge some extra business is gone. Footballers are impatient: they want everything today.

Agents get the boots from contacts at Nike, Puma, adidas or New Balance. Or just buy them from a wholesaler. But it looks better for the agent if they can demonstrate the value of their contacts at the big sportswear manufacturers without having to buy them.

Pairing up

It is an expensive business keeping players happy – even young players. Agents will try to get agreements with

All about the boot deals

Aspiring players will probably judge agents on whether they can deliver better boots. If an agent can provide boots on the day a player wants them, then that makes them a great agent. If the agent can't, then, frankly, he or she is not a good agent.

Agents can start talking to young players at 15, and sign them at 16. It used to be 18 but now there are so many agents that they've got to work that bit harder and get deals done earlier.

boot manufacturers and certainly the top agents can pick up the phone and get hold of boots, no problem. Normally, the top agents will have plenty of boots ready to dish out to the latest target, the latest player they want to sign. Some smaller agents will have a contact or two or maybe the next best thing – some sort of deal with a wholesaler to get them boots quickly and at a reduced rate. The players will be impressed at a young age if an agent can get them the latest pair.

Texting, texting

When players are young, around the ages of 14 or 15, agents will deal with their parents. The contact with the player will be limited to things like simple text messages – 'good luck for the match' or 'how did it go?' And so on. Agents cannot break the rules, and cannot sign them up before they are 16 but they will try and build up relationships to earn trust. But players up to the age of 15 cannot be signed and agents cannot make illegal or silly promises until allowed to do so.

Trust is key

It's about building trust at that age. The best agents will always say to any family,

that getting the right deal can change all of their lives, not just their son's.

If all goes well in three, four or maybe even five years they will all be in a room one day signing a contract with a club which will transform the whole family's lives.

That puts considerable expectations and responsibilities on an agent. No-one will want to be in that room, discussing a contract, negotiating big money deals for their child, and basically deciding the futures of their nearest and dearest and having to rely on intermediaries they do not 100 per cent trust.

Buy in

That's why those three or four years from 14 upwards is about building trust and relationships between player, club and agent. People either buy into those relationships or they don't. Even if they do there is little sense of permanence to it: players change their minds and after as brief a time as a year later they could be looking elsewhere for other people to represent them.

It is worth stating again: there is no loyalty, even from a young age. In fact, at a guess around 60 per cent – and that's the absolute minimum – of players would say: 'I'm not really bothered about my agent. He's alright.' That does not encourage long-term relationships. There is an absence of long-term commitment and players chop and change all the time.

That's why it's vital to forge trust, and build a relationship so that at 16 when the best kids are able and ready to sign a deal they'll do it with you.

Education, education, education

The clubs will tell the best players at 14 what they stand to earn if they progress and get to sign their first professional contract at 16. That can be £8,000 or

£9,000-a-week. But at 16, the standard scholarship contract is just £120-a-week. But clubs get around it by having an agreement with the family, that they will provide incentives, such as regularly paying them £75,000-a-year or paying the family's housing expenses.

Clubs sign footballers because they are very good at football and want to make them better in order to play for their teams. That is stating the obvious and trumps all other considerations. But clubs will look after a player's whole development and education, not just his football one. Most clubs have a tie-up with private schools.

All the top Premier League clubs have arrangements for educating their players, as do clubs lower down the pyramid. Fulham do it as well.

The typical set-up is academy players go to school during the day then go to the club. They might go to school from 8am to 1pm and then straight to the training ground to be with the club. Players have to do their GCSEs and carry on their education – not that many kids maintain their standards because they all lose interest in school as soon as they sign for a club.

If not a full-time programme, such as players at a Championship club or below, they will be on day release for one, possibly two days a week.

Schooled

The game of football is increasingly supportive of all-round development of players and formal education as key. Schools themselves do not have to agree but most of them do.

Arsenal, for example, will have the scope to take players out of the classroom and on to the training pitch. The boys can catch up with their school work another time.

The problem for mum and dad is

trying to keep their child focused. It's why kids tended to leave school with poor GCSE grades. Now clubs and schools are trying a different system. They are in school every day at least, but they are also training every day. The various commitments and learning even themselves out.

The emphasis at 14, though, becomes the football. Do the players stay focused? In a word, no. When it comes to formal education they are to all intents and purposes, gone. They've given up on lessons and it's all about focus on football.

A lot of attention and fuss has been paid to Duncan Watmore at Sunderland. Famously, he has completed a degree course at university. But he's the exception to the rule. There are a large number of kids in training in professional football – and Watmore is one of the very few to carry on studying.

Scouts' honour

Agents use their contacts to find players they want to represent. They will often have links with or be tipped off by a scout. Word will come through that there's a teenager at MK Dons or Colchester, or wherever, and then if he's good enough, the agent will start the work to try to sign him.

Sixteen-year-olds at Premier League clubs are probably tapped up less than the kids of the same age at MK Dons because big clubs have obviously signed those players up already. If an agent is good enough and puts the hours in they might go to a club's under-18s game on a Saturday morning and there will be scouts from Man United, Liverpool, Man City, Tottenham or whoever. And any agent worth his salt should know who the best players and prospects are.

The scouts or reps from clubs are also

WHAT THE AGENT SAID

Sweet sixteen

Agents cannot sign a player until 1 January of their 16th year. The best youngsters at the top clubs will be signed up straight away because they will be the ones most sought after.

That said, the best youngsters at League One or League Two clubs will have agents queuing round the block. One kid, a 15-year-old called Malakai Hinckson-Mars, went from Barnet to Chelsea and there was a huge number of agents at Cobham, the Chelsea training ground, saying they were his agent. It was incredible.

looking for information. They are looking to swap info and a lot of these talent spotters are getting paid under the table by agents, or 'encouraged' in a 'you scratch my back' sort of way to divulge what they know about players. It has to be remembered a lot of these scouts are part-time workers doing full-time hours yet are only being paid a pittance. That makes it tempting for scouts to try and earn money on the side. The agent will say, 'If you give me a couple of grand I'll talk you through the best kids.' Is it illegal? Probably not. Would they take it? Almost certainly. That's how it works and, as ever in football, money makes the world go round.

There are also deals where families are cut into contracts with agents. The main one is where the agent offers a proportion of any money he makes. He might offer the family 30 per cent of anything he makes on the player from the contract negotiations, transfer fee, loyalty bonus or whatever.

It can arise whereby a club says, 'If you get us that kid, then we'll give you £30,000.' It can go far higher, obviously. But everything is above board with the agent under no illusions that he will be well recompensed if he can deliver the player they want.

Clubs and agents

Clubs have preferred agents who they push their players towards. At face value that might sound contentious but it makes sense. The clubs are right to be wary: there are some unscrupulous characters about and so they encourage players to sign with an agent they trust and like.

The problem is that then breeds suspicion and disquiet. Agents outside of that cosy arrangement, whether they are good agents or not, will get annoyed, and that creates its own problems. Accusations of favouritism will fly and tensions can mount. Suddenly, relationships built up down the years where one agent will point players towards one club can be at risk. Everyone has to be kept sweet. Maybe someone at the club is on the payroll.

The evidence for this is clear if you know where to look. It can be seen when certain players sign on with certain agents who have big links to particular clubs and the player joins those clubs. It is an old pals' act within football.

Football is a little bit in the dark ages like that. The FA, the clubs, the owners, are caught in a time warp.

Money changers

Officially, young players are not allowed to go on secret tours of training grounds. Nor are their families. It's not allowed – but it happens every single day. It is impossible to stop.

How can a kid be stopped from going to a training ground? How can a parent be watched to make sure he doesn't take the day off work to visit a club? It's not practical, not to say illegal.

So many of football's rules and regulations are broken. The reality is that throughout football, rules have to be bent, otherwise no deal would ever get done. Clubs and agents must know in advance if a player is willing to move or another club is willing to sell, unless they are contacted and asked.

From the perspective of the player, such concerns are not really important. The end game is the only thing that matters to them. As long as they reach the top and make a lot of money, then they don't really care how it's done.

There's a few young players who have been caught up in rows between agents. Some stories have made the papers and even created some unwanted headlines. But it is highly unlikely to affect them in the long term or even the short term.

The amount of money that changes hands among agents is incredible. There is a growing trend for agents or agencies paying to sign players without any serious diligence. The agency has not scouted a player, watched him, nor gone to meeting after meeting about him. They've just paid for him. It's as simple as that. Agents are just gambling on signing up players in the hope they come good.

Much of the time an agent will offer to pay big money to the dad. That's not necessarily the best thing for a footballer. But it's part and parcel of the industry now. It probably doesn't affect the player. They don't care. The family has made money and a new agent has taken over. 'Hello, come meet your new agent.' It is as simple as that.

Six figures for every deal

In any walk of life or in any industry, expertise is essential, and that applies to football agency, too. It's similar to being a journalist. Anyone can say they are a journalist, write a story and try to sell it. But the work is not as good as that which an experienced journalist can deliver. Similarly with skilled trades like carpentry or plumbing. Amateurs can have a go. But no one would want to rely on their work.

It's the same as being an agent. The good, experienced agent knows the game, knows how to operate. Yet some of the new agents who have no experience or expertise simply go around paying for players.

The top agents will want at least six figures for any deal they are involved, whether they're moving players from

Burnley or Scunthorpe. They would not, as the cliché goes, get out of bed for less.

Club versus country – at 14

The best players will be called up by England or whichever country they represent. They will love it – and the clubs absolutely hate it.

Why? Because the clubs don't want their best young players going away, getting their heads turned, gossiping with other kids, the rivalry, potentially getting tapped up. Or even worse injured.

Even at a young age, the whole club versus country debate is quickly established. But it's very prestigious and again it comes down to one-upmanship. It's all about showing off, getting called up, playing for your country and the FA are buying into it more than ever.

And if you go on Twitter or Instagram, you will see how much the kids love being called up by England. They see it as a huge step in their career and something to show off about to their mates.

If you are going to be a top player then you want to say you've been called up by the under-16s, they love it. The under-17s, 19s and even the 20s have all had success with England and the players love being part of it.

The FA and talent scouts are watching games every Saturday and Sunday, to see if there are kids out there to come into the system. The FA are moving away from traditional scouting in their Talent ID set-up towards statistics. It's a move towards the modern world.

But it overlooks the fact that England and the FA have had tremendous success through the age groups from the under-17s up to the under-20s, both winning the World Cup at their respective age groups in 2017.

◄◄ ▬▬▬▬
Manchester United manager Jose Mourinho keeps his younger players close to hand to soak up the atmosphere. (Getty)

06

THE TRUTH ABOUT YOUTH

The way young players come through the ranks is in the process of being revolutionised. And the revolution is being increasingly televised, thanks to more channels showing competitions like the Youth Cup. That should be a good thing, showcasing the stars of tomorrow as they develop. There is no set way of making the grade as a young player. But one thing's for sure: there has never been as much debate about whether the current youth system is failing our young players and if enough players are coming through.

The way we were

In recent years, big clubs have farmed out players to smaller clubs in the emergency loan-market system. It meant players could move from Premier League clubs to the Championship or wherever outside of the transfer windows.

Premier League clubs liked it because their players got first team experience, and some grounding in men's football – real football, which the under-21s league just does not offer.

Top managers have been queuing up to criticise the under-21s league because it does not offer decent competition to players. It's just a kick-about between youngsters, and does not get them remotely ready for senior competitive football.

Loan deals do still exist, and they work. That's why the best young players like Daniel Sturridge or Jack Wilshere were farmed out on loan to clubs like Bolton. Even David Beckham went to Preston and Frank Lampard had a spell at Swansea.

Daniel Sturridge playing for England, proving that being loaned out does your football hopes no harm. (Shutterstock)

More recently, others like Harry Kane, for example, have made the grade after being sent out on loan. They get a football education outside of the pampered world of the Premier League.

Under-performing under-21s

Loan deals down the years have been a familiar path used by some of the biggest names. But the problem is that FIFA have insisted the Premier League and Football League fall into line with the rest of football and had to scrap the emergency-loan market and that will mean players can only move in transfer windows whereas before loan deals could be agreed even when the window was shut. This is a major setback for players because, in the past, players could be loaned out during the season, they could play games, play in competitive football and it would really help their development. Now if they do not move then sometimes they can be stuck, hardly playing any games, until the next window opens and valuable months can be lost in their progression.

This is part of the problem and contributes to worrying times for youth development. Some kids will be fast-tracked straight into the first team while others will be left to languish on the bench, stuck playing under-23s football or, even worse, not get any game time at all. In the old system, lower clubs would be grateful to sign them and they would get game time. Just look at how loans have helped the likes of Harry Kane and Andros Townsend.

Second rate

The other worry is that football generally has lost faith in the under-21s league which is often played out by second-rate youngsters because the best ones have been loaned out or are in the first team anyway. Historically, players would cut their teeth in the youth team, become men in the reserves side and then step up into the first team. Now the Premier League II is supposed to bridge the gap but many in football think it is a very poor competition and is one of the factors as to why more kids are not coming through.

The Premier League has tried various ways to improve youth development and, in particular, the Premier League II which is under-23s now. Those ideas include televising games to increase the profile and interest while there is bigger

CHELSEA FOOTBALL CLUB

prize money on offer – as much as £3m to the winners – to make sure clubs take it more seriously and use it for youth development. But the problem is that the games lack intensity, they lack physicality and often they look like training ground exercises. The best kids play the best kids and they knock it around very nicely but rarely do you see tough games that really push players.

Toughen up

All the big clubs set up loan deals. They decide where their players go. They loan them out and place them very carefully.

When Patrick Bamford was at Chelsea he was not sure about the wisdom of going on loan to Middlesbrough but the then boss at the Riverside, Aitor Karanka, is Jose Mourinho's close friend (Mourinho being Chelsea manager at the time). So Bamford was assured by

those connections that his career would develop positively with the loan deal, and it arguably has, since Bamford later signed on a permanent deal with Boro.

Going Dutch

There has also been a regular supply line of Chelsea kids going to Holland to join Vitesse Arnhem. It's a brilliant experience for them and it's something that Chelsea do really well. It's not always a guarantee for them to get through into the first team but in terms of building a young player's career then it's something they do brilliantly.

Faced with the prospect of being sent on loan, an 18-year-old player might ask his agent's opinion. But, for a kid in League One for example, then they might be loaned out to a non-league club well down the pyramid. Some players might see that as an insult. But it shouldn't be. It is part of a footballer's education and a

▼

Patrick Bamford signed for Chelsea, but was put on loan which put him on another club career path. (Getty)

◄◄

Being loaned has aided Andros Townsend in furthering his chances of Premier League action. (Shutterstock)

Old versus new – Bobby Charlton and David Beckham compare England kits. Beckham, on his way to stardom, was loaned to Preston. (Getty)

valuable lesson in how to cope and how to play adult football. It helps teenagers to toughen up and get ready for a big career in the game where players cannot afford not to be tough.

If it's good enough for Becks...

The biggest celebrity in football, David Beckham, went on loan to Preston. David Beckham was not the best footballer of all time, but he became the biggest star at one stage, made the most money and earned over 100 England caps. He made the most of his career and his talent through sheer hard work, determination and an incredible attitude.

But Beckham was not fast-tracked into the Manchester United first team. He came through at Old Trafford after a loan spell at 'lowly' Preston. If he had to go out on loan, why shouldn't anyone else? The loan market is purely about learning how to play and how to cope with men's football. It's about becoming a man.

Odd games

Going to learn about men's football to then come back and play in the first team is a logical move. A more recent example is that of Arsenal with a player like Chuba Akpom. He has had a whole series of loan spells from Brentford to Brighton, with Coventry and Hull City in between. Regular games in the Championship was better for his development than staying at the Emirates and getting a game in the odd cup tie or the odd two-minute run-out as a substitute.

For some players it is also about developing life skills, how to behave, how to act in the first team dressing room and, along the way, learning some important lessons.

The enforcers

Every club has an enforcer. If any player steps out of line, 'the enforcer' will ensure everything is sorted out. And *really* sorted out. Any transgressors – disruptive influences, troublemakers, or players who are not pulling for the team – will be pulled into line.

Someone who knows a thing or two about the loan system is Chuba Akpom. (Getty)

Dutch club Vitesse Arnhem is a good platform for some Chelsea youngsters. (Shutterstock)

The prime example of this is Roy Keane. It is hard to imagine any cocky young player giving Keane any backchat and getting away with it. While Keane has been very much his own man, there's a 'Roy Keane' at every club, a leader in the dressing room. Damien Delaney at Crystal Palace is one such example. Everyone listens when he barks out his orders. He soon pulls people into line.

Every dressing room needs to have someone saying: 'This is our way – buy into it, or f*** off.' It is rarely the best player, but it is generally the best personality because they'll be loud, strong and determined. Young players learn from these experienced pros, especially when they go on loan.

Over the line

Another great example is Benik Afobe. When he was 16 and coming through the ranks at Arsenal, he was being trailed as the next Thierry Henry. Afobe is big, strong and when he was playing for Arsenal under-18s, he seemed to score four goals every game. Goals, goals, goals. He was pushing for consideration every week, making great strides and progressing to the under-21s. But then he couldn't quite get over the line and make a first-team breakthrough. He

went out on loan a couple of times, but without real success. Arsenal let him go on a number of loans, including to MK Dons where he scored goals, before leaving on a permanent deal to Wolves, and then Bournemouth for just over £11m – then back to Wolves and on loan to Stoke.

Playing with experienced pros and leaders on loan, shaped Afobe into a player good enough to play at the elite level. He could have stayed at Arsenal but not made it into the first team. He wouldn't have been a main man at Arsenal. And, of course, he will have made big money from the transfer fees he has commanded.

Another consequence is that players have graduated from Arsenal's youth system. It might not be with the Gunners but the club has produced players good enough for the Premier League. It's the same at Tottenham, Man United, Chelsea or other elite clubs: people say they don't produce kids. The fact is they do make good careers for these youngsters.

Producing players

Parents thinking of taking their child to Chelsea or Arsenal, are often heard to comment, 'They don't get the kids through, do they?' The truth is that they do. Arsenal

The versatile and talented Benik Afobe. (Getty)

can cite Afobe. He didn't make it at the Emirates, but he could be sold for £15m and his experience shows that the Gunners do produce footballers. It shows that there is a pathway to first-team football, even if it might not be with them. They receive a great schooling, they train at a top club and they've got a great chance to make a great career. Much criticism has been levelled at Chelsea, with over 30 young players out on loan. But many of them will have the chance of a successful and lucrative career via Stamford Bridge.

Pub talk

Of course the parents can be just as vain as their children. When the dad is down the pub on a Saturday night, he can boast: 'My son is at Arsenal. Where's your boy? Charlton?' It is a big put-down and the son's ties with Arsenal provide the parent with a status symbol.

When Benik Afobe was 16 and making incredible progress at Arsenal, the idea that he'd be on loan in League One in two or three years' time would have been seen as a negative. Players in that situation and their parents will become disenchanted and insist that their son will make it at the big club.

For someone in Afobe's situation, now he's matured, he can see the bigger picture, and that it's a better scenario for him with the way it's worked out.

There is an idea that the leagues and governing bodies should make it compulsory to have one home-grown player on the bench. This would give every player a chance or at least a bit of hope of progression. If they don't get that, they can lose hope and inspiration and fade away.

Paths to success

Mauricio Pochettino at Tottenham brought through young English players like Dele Alli, Danny Rose, Harry Winks and Harry Kane. Tottenham developed a great presence in the England squad. It proves that young English players can progress to the national side via a Premier League club.

Football is not just about the club pathway. It should be about whether there's a football pathway as a whole, somewhere which can take a player onto having a good career regardless of which club he starts at.

Reality bites

The older, better and more experienced agents will preach that kind of pathway. They will make it clear that dropping out, or being loaned out of a big club, is not necessarily the end. The newer, less experienced agents might see it as failure. Their reasoning is to get their clients to

sign with the big clubs, seeing that as the true measure of success. Some agents will be scared to say anything else other than they can get a player to a top club. The family will not want to hear the reality. If an agent says he cannot secure places at a top club, but another says he can, then the family will probably sign for the agent who makes all the promises even if he can't deliver. Even he might know he can't. But somewhere down the line the reality bites and the agent does not want to admit that he'll also have to consider placing the young player at a lesser club.

Lucrative

The agents with integrity and brutal honesty will tell the truth from the outset. Agents have to be truthful because it's important to show and tell people that it's not just about the club. It's also about knowing there is a pathway into making a good career. Jamie Vardy, Charlie Austin and Benik Afobe prove there is. They may well be millionaires already, but their next big deal will definitely make them a millionaire. Any prospective player who has a problem with that really needs to re-evaluate. Players who do not make it at a big club can still have very good and lucrative careers.

All in the mind

Harry Kane is an example of another pathway. He went on so many loans – to Millwall, Orient, Norwich and Leicester. He hardly set the world alight at any of them, but Mauricio Pochettino gave him a chance. And just look at Kane now.

His agent would have had a say on where he went on loan. They would identify a good club, ask where he is going to play and consider the style of play at the clubs he was loaned to. For a

Before settling into a more permanent role at Spurs, Harry Kane was sent out on loan.
(Shutterstock)

player to go somewhere on loan and then not play at that club is the worst feeling of all and it can really set the player back. But Kane dropped down, went out on loan to the right clubs and gained invaluable experience.

Kane has huge confidence and belief. He was convinced he would make it, and worked damn hard to ensure he did. But whatever the pathway, whether it's a scholarship, a pro contract, loans or dropping down the divisions, the players who make a career in the game refuse to be told that they're not good enough. Because if they were not good enough they would not have already made it so far and be in with a chance in any case.

Belief

So the difference between taking that ability and getting into the first team is largely in the head. It's about players believing in themselves and having confidence. Potential players simply would not get a pro contract unless

the club believed in them and that they have a chance.

They would not pay a young player – whether it is £500-a-week or £8,000-a-week – if they were not good enough. The club believe players can make it.

No easy solution

It's hard to know what can really be the overall solution for youth football and bringing kids through. Closing the

WHAT THE AGENT SAID

Last laughs

Some kids do get fed up. One young lad, a 16-year-old, who was at a Premier League club, dropped down to a big club in the Championship. He just rang his agent one day and said: 'I want to leave, I'm 16, in my first year, I'm not playing, there are new players coming in. I get overlooked, the local lads get overlooked for the foreigners and I don't want to be here.'

The kid went to a Championship club and he was put in their first team squad. All his mates at the original Premier League club were laughing at him. But when the two clubs eventually played each other, the kids who used to take the mickey out of him were sitting there in the stands watching him play. He had the last laugh.

That kind of situation won't suit everyone. Sometimes if a player is young and very good, then it might be better for his development for him to stay at the elite club and train with elite players. But what is perceived to be a step down can mean a player is getting actual game time rather than being stuck in a big queue to try and get game time at the parent club.

There's a player in League Two. He's a decent forward, playing in the No10 role. He's 17, playing first-team football and being watched by 35 scouts. Half of the Championship clubs and the bottom half of the Premier League are watching him because he's playing every week at 17. That's a worthwhile pathway.

emergency-loan market might be a huge blow for youth development and it could really hurt players, clubs and agents.

But the problem with the under-21s is the intensity. There is such a difference to the Premier League. Managers have careers that are so short-lived now. They cannot gamble on putting kids in so the kids don't get a chance.

Greg Dyke, when he was FA chairman, wanted to introduce a scheme whereby managers would provide opportunities for young players on a more formal, regulated basis like quotas or even B teams playing in the lower divisions.

But for players in the under-23s league, because the intensity is so different, then it's hard to know if they're ready for the first team.

It's also hard for youngsters to get a break and play in the first team when there are so many clubs fielding teams virtually entirely made up of established and relatively more experienced foreign players bought for substantial fees.

Value for money

Everyone has got huge admiration for what Stoke City and their manager Mark Hughes did. But three of the best players in the team had been Marko Arnautovic, Bojan and Xherdan Shaqiri, for which Stoke paid a grand total of about £20m for all three.

British players, with half of their ability, would cost £60m. Were he British, Shaqiri would have cost £25m or £30m. Stoke took a chance on Bojan, a brilliant player, but one who had a major injury at Barcelona. Stoke would argue they took a chance on him. But were he English he would have cost upwards of £30m.

Compare that to Charlie Adam, bought by Stoke for £13m. Adam is a good player and was brilliant at Blackpool because he

learn from him. Or at least that is what Chelsea thought. But they sent him out on loan, he lost confidence and he was eventually moved on. He is a shadow of the player he once was.

It is such a shame. It is also a great example of a young player who should be in a far better position than he is. But because of the influx of foreign players into this country, it supports the theory that the development of the best English kids is stunted. That's why the loan market must stay intact as it provides great opportunities, many clubs use it well and it helps young players develop.

ran that team, but £13m at the time was a big price. Foreign talent purchased off the peg represents better value. That's why for the young players, it's so depressing. Because it means a big obstacle is placed in their pathway.

Stunted progress

Chelsea will champion the fact that they have a large number of players out on loan. The challenge from critics is that surely a few more of them could have had careers at Chelsea but because they keep buying foreign players the policy has stunted the progress of their youth-team players.

The career of the footballer is so dependent on the platform and opportunity.

Take Josh McEachran, one of Chelsea's more high-profile examples of their youth policy in recent years. At 17, he was in the Chelsea first team squad and very highly rated. He went to West London neighbours Brentford, playing in the Championship. Does this reflect poorly on Chelsea or the player?

There is an argument that because Chelsea were not sure about playing a teenager every week, they simply went out and spent £40m on a midfielder. McEachran could sit on the bench and

Too much too young

As previously noted at 16, all players want is boots. By the time they reach 18, they start to get obsessed with cars. They are paid too much money, far too much money. And the biggest danger is that all this new-found wealth means they lose their appetite. It is hard to argue against that. That's where the game is going wrong. Clubs should not be paying a 17-or 18-year-old – unless he's playing regular first team football – £10,000-a-week, not even £5,000-a-week. If they become millionaires overnight then surely that will affect their desire and commitment if they feel they have already reached the top. That's why so many promising players fall by the wayside after being caught up in the 'too much, too young' trap. It is hard to comprehend that sort of money at that age. Where does the hunger go? It kills it.

Hunger and desire

By the time a player is 18, if he has been offered a professional contract, whether it's Premier League or League Two, it shows he is good enough to play

That desire can quickly get dampened by someone giving a player half a million pounds a year because it makes life so easy. If a youngster is earning £30,000-a-year or £40,000-a-year, which is a lot of money for any 17-or 18-year-old, then the hunger and desire is still there. If youngsters see the big-name pros coming in every day in their Ferraris then it encourages them to think: 'I can get there, I can get that.' But if the kid is earning £250,000-a-year then he can afford a Ferrari. So what's the point? They've got it all already.

Football eats itself

No-one is big enough at the FA to admit it or do anything but football is in danger of eating itself. They all talk about 2022 and winning the World Cup and that being the target for the next generation. But no-one is bold enough to say there is a major problem in youth development so the promising kids may never come through or realise their potential.

Stay hungry

Some will argue that it's not possible to coach or teach hunger and desire. But one thing's for certain, it can certainly be taken away by making things too easy.

If an individual wants something that much then they will go out and chase it. If he has been given it too easily, then he won't show enough attitude and desire. If a player is not playing in the first team and yet still earning fortunes, his desire might decline. It is in the interests of players and clubs to keep that hunger – and fat contracts aren't the thing to make a person hungry.

But some agents are part of the problem. They come along promising to move players. Why, at the age of 18

Coming through the ranks of a big club like Chelsea doesn't always guarantee a long-term stay, as Josh McEachran found out. (Shutterstock)

professional football. Because he would not be offered a professional contract when he is 18 if he did not have the technical ability.

Whether it's Manchester United or Mansfield Town, they are not giving a contract to an 18-year-old who is not technically good enough to be a professional footballer.

To get over that threshold and become a pro, it is all about what's in your head. Forget technical ability. All young players in the system have got that. It is about showing hunger, desire and determination. Attitude and the general mental strength to show that you are better than the player in front of you. Keep showing that desire.

💬 WHAT THE AGENT SAID

Bad advice

There was one 16-year-old, regarded as one of the best prospects in the country, who was at a big club. He was years ahead of his age groups. Then an unscrupulous agent got greedy, wanted to get big money out of a club and told the player to start making big demands. The club then got worried. They could see it all going wrong and next thing you know they were showing him the door rather than giving him a new contract.

He went to another club. He still wants to be a footballer, but at 16, he was getting bad advice and agents were telling him he should be earning the same as the first team players.

There was another kid taken out of a good club in the Premier League, moved abroad, and he's now playing in their reserves. Where has his career gone? That's not an example of good advice from an agent. It's just greed. They have been impatient and put financial rewards first, ahead of the player's best interests. This kind of behaviour is ruining players' careers.

Young kids are asking for too much, the agents are telling them to demand £500,000, insisting on big agent fees and it is all so wrong. The bad agents get in their clients' heads and ruin them.

Some kids are heading off the rails of their own accord. But that is when an agent should be trying to guide them, take them in the right direction, not make them even more greedy.

There was even a story in one newspaper of a kid who went into training one day at his club wearing the scarf of another team. Who told him to do that? The agent. Why? Because he said it would prove that he was thinking about joining the other club to try and blackmail his current club to give him more money.

He walked through the gates of the training ground with a scarf of another team, went into the dressing room and sat down. He knew everyone was looking and yet his agent told him to do it.

He was 16 and when someone is telling you that he can move you to another club and treble your wages, then you're going to do it. The sad truth is that he got kicked out of the club, no-one signed him, and he was left without a club.

Another agent got him and went to other clubs, asked for stupid money and no-one wanted to touch him. It was madness. Everyone knew he'd been thrown out, that he was a problem, and yet his agents were still asking for crazy money. No-one was going to pay it.

or 19, would a youngster want to leave a top club? Why would they listen to an incompetent, self-serving agent promising a move to a second-rate club with the option that in a year the player can come back? Why? Because of money. Yet players should not be worrying about money at that age.

Stay put and stay focused

Young players always get frustrated. Suddenly they want to move and that's when the best advice can be to tell them to stay focused, sit tight and ignore anyone getting in their ear telling them to cause unrest and move. It's such an important time for young players and one bad move can kill a youngster's career.

Greed is not good

That's why we've got so many problems, why so many kids won't make it, why greed is such a problem in the game. It is important that people know that and also that people know just how bad some agents are for young players. It is sheer greed. This is about the mapping of a young player's career. This is about the life, soul and career of a young player and developing into a professional footballer, and it can go badly awry.

Overpriced assets

Domestic players have become a ridiculously overpriced commodity in the market. Whether they are 16 or 30, they have become an asset that costs far too much and that is a major issue for the game.

It is a serious problem that impacts significantly. Take the example of Aston Villa, who were relegated from the Premier

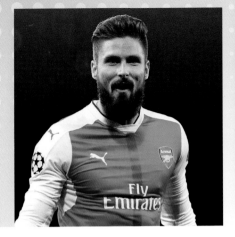

◄◄◄ ▬▬▬
French player Olivier
Giroud and Andy
Carroll from England.
Who is the better bet?
(Shutterstock)

League in the 2015/16 season. They needed experience for a relegation fight, but instead they brought in inexperienced foreign youngsters. That's the last thing they needed. But someone clearly did not feel that English players were a good buy either because they were not good enough, were overpriced or had the wrong attitude.

Villa brought in a whole raft of foreign players – and went down. It was a false economy to rationalise making savings by buying from abroad but it was counter-productive. They tried to save money by going foreign – and it ended up costing them big time.

Finding the next generation

For Premier League clubs with the ability to pay huge wages thanks to the lucrative TV deals, it is easy to go into the market, sign three or four kids from Germany, France or wherever, for next to nothing. Clubs hope one of these players makes it, but they are not particularly bothered about the other five. Because in terms relative to buying British players, it costs next to nothing.

There must be a greater emphasis on British, home-grown players if football is to help the Home Nations and their national teams. It is becoming harder and harder

for young British players to make it in large part because of the influx of the average foreign players. Not top level talent, just average ones. That persists across all age levels.

Giroud v Carroll

A good example of how the economics work is when Arsenal paid £11m for Olivier Giroud. A French international and proven goal scorer in Ligue 1, he joined the Gunners after Montpellier had won the championship.

Compare that to Andy Carroll, who commanded a £35m fee when he went from Newcastle to Liverpool and another big fee when he joined West Ham. How was that justified? Because he's English. In football circles, English players are seen as safe bets, more reliable and also help the English quota in the squad. Even though Giroud was a France international, he was seen as a bigger gamble than Carroll. And if you look at how it worked out, Arsenal got much better value.

The commodity value of the English player is being driven to stratospheric heights and it is stunting the growth of footballers in this country. It makes the domestic league more of a European game and kills the development of the young player.

Fewer opportunities

The wholesale signing of players from foreign academies is the biggest danger to young British kids coming through and becoming superstars of the future. Arsenal have been doing it for years, from Cesc Fabregas through to Hector Bellerin. Across the game some of these strategies work, but there are plenty more examples that have not.

The consequence is that big clubs will sign foreign kids at 16 rather than look for talent at places like Hartlepool, Colchester or Blackpool, to try to find the best British kids. It means fewer and fewer home-grown players come through and it makes it tougher for youngsters to make the grade. They are now up against not just other British kids but the best youngsters from all over the world.

Becoming a professional footballer has never been tougher – and it will only get harder. It is difficult to know for certain whether, when Arsenal signed Hector Bellerin at 16, there was not another right back in Britain who had the same potential. If the home-grown British player had been given the same coaching opportunities and platform then maybe he would be better than Bellerin. But that is conjecture. We will never know, now.

A Premier League star – after only 30 games

As soon as Demarai Gray got into the first team at Birmingham, he was being tipped for the Premier League. He had not played 30 games and suddenly he was being talked about as being a Premier League player. Why? Because he's got talent but also because he was being pushed and marketed. His debut got him into the public consciousness. It ended up getting him a big money move to Leicester City.

There was another youngster, James Maddison, who was at Coventry. As soon as he was in the team, he was being touted for Manchester City or Liverpool or Spurs. Norwich came in on deadline day and probably paid what was an inflated fee just

WHAT THE AGENT SAID

There's always a way to get paid

But whatever kind of player, English or foreign, there is lots of money to be made. All these deals are very lucrative for agents. A player can move from a Championship club to a top Premier League club and the agent will earn £200,000. That is not exceptional by any means. It's a run-of-the-mill deal.

Obviously agents are not supposed to represent kids and earn from deals at a young age, but there are ways and means around.

A clause can be put in the contract that the agent's fee is paid when the player turns 18. Or the agent can be paid by being described as a scout or a consultant. There is always a way, even if the FA are trying to weed those sort of payments out.

As soon as a player gets in the first team at a Premier League club, the tapping up begins. It can be from a Championship club, League One or another Premier League club: the approaches come from all angles.

A hypothetical scenario is one whereby a young player has just made his debut for Crystal Palace. His agent will be ringing up the representatives of Arsenal, Chelsea and Manchester City to say: 'Have you seen him? Have a look.' It's done to get his name out there, put his name on people's radars and get him into people's minds.

to get him on their books. His next move was interesting to watch with Leicester City offering in the region of £22m for him.

Cashing in

That deal suited all parties because the player got his next move, Norwich likely pocketed a big profit and Coventry cashed in as well due to sell-on clauses.

Coventry were actively looking to sell Maddison during the January window in 2016. A British player is a valuable commodity, and if the comparison is made between James Maddison at Coventry or some youngster in Germany, Maddison will cost three or four times as much. It makes no sense but there is a huge premium for British players.

Small fees, big profits

A lot of Championship and League One clubs scout for players from non-league and countries like Ireland. Peterborough are a great example. They signed Conor Washington for £500,000 from Newport, then sold him for nearly £3m two years later to QPR. A huge profit. That model works for Peterborough because they exploit their status as a club that has played in the Championship and therefore can say the player scored at a good level. It is highly unlikely Conor Washington would have been worth £2.5m or £3m in the second or third division in Spain.

Second-rate millionaires

Germany, Spain and Italy are England's biggest rivals in terms of leagues. Clubs in those countries would not pay a fraction of what English ones do for players in domestic moves.

Serie B has a salary cap. Players are on small amounts and it's tiny compared to the rest of the top footballing nations and their second tier leagues.

Players in England can be on £28,000-a-week or more in the Championship. They are millionaires and have not even reached the top of their profession.

But the club also sees them as assets and commodities. And that means they can return a nice healthy profit if they are sold on.

The manager at a club might not even be aware that profit is due to be cashed in. The chief executive will be on the phone to another club, looking for a big pay day, and saying, 'Have you seen our kid – we can sell him for £3m.'

Once the player has hit the first team then it is open season. The player is a piece of meat and everyone is ready to do business. That's why people in or outside the game should not really think of the players as being greedy, disloyal or over-ambitious. Because clubs sell them in the blink of an eye if it's a good deal.

Demarai Gray has benefited from being tipped as a future player to look out for.
(Shutterstock)

07

DEBUTS AND DASHED DREAMS

The ultimate aim for any player must be getting into the first team, reaching the top and maybe even playing for a national side. After all, that is why most youngsters started playing football, what they dreamed of when they were kicking the ball around in the playground all those years ago. But, sadly, by the time some of those kids have grown up and broken into the first team, a bit of that magic has already gone. They have lost the wide-eyed schoolboy dream when it was all about the glory of scoring the last-minute winner in the Cup Final. For many, that has long since disappeared with the greed, jealousy and underhand nature that ruins what was once called the beautiful game.

Pride and prejudice

The day when a footballer finally crosses the white line and makes his debut after all the years of hard work, should be the proudest moment for everyone concerned. The player himself, the family, his friends and, of course, all those that have already latched on to him, trying to get a piece of the action and a share of the rewards.

The genuine people with the player's interests at heart will feel 10 feet tall, so proud and so happy that he has made the grade. The ones who are not genuine will not be worried about the debut. They will already be thinking about the next step, the next move and how to get there quickly.

All about money (again)

When a player makes his debut, it's worth having a look at the people around him already. Like those agents who are not bothered about the player, and are just concerned about making money – and as much of it as possible.

As with any profession, there are good people and there are bad ones.

The good ones will be bursting with pride when a young player gets into the first team. It will be a day to savour. They will be happy that they've played a part.

For the bad ones, they are not bothered about debuts and emotional moments like that. They're just interested in it being another step on the ladder – another chance to make money.

••• WHAT THE AGENT SAID

What's in it for the scouts?

Talent spotting might sound glamorous and lucrative but the reality is much more prosaic, even at the big clubs. Chelsea's scouts for the academy alone, are all part-time. There can be up to 60 of them going to games all of the time.

The scouts might be part-time but they could get around £25,000-a-year on top of their ordinary jobs, and others might get bonuses if the players make it. But go down to lesser levels and some scouts don't get paid at all, or just receive mileage allowance and minimal expenses.

Sadly, getting a player into the first team or to be playing for a national side isn't the ultimate aim for a lot of agents. It's all about the money. And they couldn't give a damn how they get it.

They are not even interested in what the player earns, either. They don't care about getting the player a good contract. Their first priority is to make sure they get a big cut, a big agent's fee, bonuses and a big slice of the pie.

There are so many who are like that. Some of these guys don't give a damn about the players. And that can be a young agent, a pushy agent, or an older agent who has got a lot of big players. Somewhere along the way, they stopped worrying about the player – and just started thinking about the cash. And if the player cannot earn them the cash then the agent will dump him.

Out of non-league and into the England team

The best stories are the ones that surprise. Not so much the kids that have come

💬 WHAT THE AGENT SAID

'Banned from every training ground in London'

There is a story of one agent who, after thinking one of his up-and-coming young players was going to sign for another agent, leaked a story about the youngster which quickly led to him being shown the door.

There is an agent who is banned from nearly every training ground in London because he targets young kids, particularly vulnerable ones from abroad. This is obviously a very sensitive subject at a time when issues of child protection and ensuring the safety and well-being of children should be of the utmost importance to those running the game and the clubs.

This disreputable agent cares not for such sensitivities. He gets 'into' the heads of impressionable youngsters, tells them he can earn them money, and is disruptive so he can move them on to other clubs. The clubs don't like it. He is not waiting around for the kid to make his debut. If one club isn't putting him in the first team fast enough, then he'll move him on to the next club whether it's good for his career and development or not.

There are lots of examples like that – far too many. It is frightening. It's not just about players being restless and pushing for moves when they're big stars in the Premier League. Increasingly, agents are pushing them even before they have made the first team. It's another huge danger for the kids of today and bright hopes of tomorrow.

For the better agents, the patient ones, the ones who care, there's a sense of pride – massive pride – to see a young player breaking into the first team. It is what a good agent wants from a career and what they set out to do. Aside from making a living for themselves, that is their ultimate goal. Nothing quite beats getting a young player through and playing first team football. If only it was like that for all of the agents. But, sadly, it definitely is not like that for a lot of them.

through the system and who were always destined to make the first team. The better tales are of someone who looked like he would never make it but has managed to play Premier League football and gone on to have a great career. The ones who were written off – the ones who most people didn't think would ever cross that white line and play professionally for a club.

Down the years, there have been some great examples. Stuart Pearce came out of non-league with Wealdstone after failing to make it at QPR. He played part-time and worked as an electrician. That gave him perspective and he had incredible enthusiasm and spirit. That sort of desire took him to the very top with Nottingham Forest and, more memorably, with England. That was all about desire.

There are many other examples of players who were at a big club, were released and yet still came back and played in the Premier League. There are plenty more good players who came through against all of the odds lower down the system.

For any agent, it's great to sign a kid at 16, help him develop and get him into the first team. Sadly, nowadays, agents probably don't expect it to happen because they are expecting the player to leave them and sign with someone else. That is the truth, unfortunately.

The buzz

For many agents there's a buzz around having the player of the moment, the current rising star, the one everyone is after. Go into boardrooms before big games and there's a player that everyone is talking about. People are going up to the agent and saying: 'Is he your player? Are you his agent?' It's a good feeling. Everyone wants to talk to you, the player is red-hot, it gives everyone around him a sense of pride. It's a good sign, shows that the agent is good at his or her job.

Sadly it seems to be the rarity nowadays. Too often now, instead of seeing happy faces in the boardroom, there are squabbles in the background, usually over money. An agent will be bickering over his slice of the pie, the family arguing, wanting some more money and the player also agitating to get himself a better deal. Like everyone else, players do not show as much loyalty, so they are looking to leave their agent and sign for another. They are less patient, in a hurry to move. The schoolboy dream of coming through, making their way up and then playing in the first team seems less special these days.

Stuart Pearce (centre), training with West Ham, worked his way up to become a faithful member of the England football team. (Getty)

Local boy made good

It was great to see Ross Barkley coming through at Everton after he had broken his leg just before he was due to break into the first team. He recovered, worked hard and when he finally made his debut it was very touching to see him pay tribute to his mum and then play for his boyhood heroes. It was a heart-warming story. But for every Barkley, there are probably 10 others who have succumbed to the growing pressures around them. They have lost the dream they had in the playground of coming through the ranks and playing for their childhood team with their heroes as teammates.

There are so many who will have ditched their agent. Their parents will have fallen out because of the pressure or a big contract, while the player has been sulking because he has not got into the first team quick enough and has been getting agitated about leaving.

The way a footballer has evolved in the last decade has changed so much and that is due to the money involved. The local boy made good, growing up and playing for the team he supports does not happen as much now. That is not enough for a kid with dreams of making it big and earning even bigger money.

There are also the age-old challenges about being the right physical size, having the right characteristics, knowing the game and tactics to make it through from being a kid and getting into the first team. Those obstacles are still to be overcome. But money has clouded the situation and made things even more difficult and fraught.

Size still matters – in England

The idea that making it as a professional footballer is all about ability and natural skill is just a myth. Most people have accepted that by now, but rather than seeing a shift towards skill over physique, the path to success is as clearly defined as it ever was and still great store is placed on strength, height and raw athletic power.

Sadly, in England the stigma remains about small players. The contrast with, for example, Spain is stark. There, the smaller players not only make it. They are prized as the model of what a really good player should be like. Several Spanish footballers have gone on to become the best players in the world, including Xavi, Iniesta, David Silva and, though not Spanish but having grown up there, Lionel Messi.

Spanish youth coaches will often suggest that coaching is viewed very differently there to how it is seen in England. From the ages of eight to 10, 90 per cent of training is based on attacking. From 10 to 12 it's 80 per cent and the rest is on the defensive side of the game and things like tackling. From 12 to 14 the ratio is 70:30, 14 to 16 it's 60:40 and at 18 it is 50:50. The emphasis in Spain is clearly on attacking and developing skills on how to pro-actively win games. That is their whole mindset: attacking players, technique, trying to score goals.

Spot the big guy?
Per Mertesacker of
Arsenal trains with
his 'average height'
team. (Getty)

It is changing here in England, pushing it towards the attacking style of play, but most still believe there's a stigma on size in this country. The game in this country is so physical and so physically demanding. The English game for years has put emphasis on physical attributes and for players to be big and strong over small, technically skilful players.

A lot of scouts, agents and even managers in Britain still believe a player has to be a certain size to be a goalkeeper in English football, and it tends to be the same for a centre half. Some managers will not sign a goalkeeper unless he is at least 6ft 2in.

Players v athletes

Arsène Wenger often said that if you gave him an athlete then he can make him a footballer. But you can't do it the other way round. So much of the prevalent attitudes in English football are about size, physique and strength.

And that was coming from Wenger, a very sophisticated and intelligent Frenchman who as a manager prided himself on style, playing with skilful, technical players and providing entertainment. Yet times are slowly changing. Take one look at how Wenger's teams evolved through the years and it is possible to see the transition between him favouring big, strapping giants who are athletes into preferring smaller, more technical players. Early Wenger Arsenal sides had the likes of Patrick Vieira and Manu Petit running the midfield. It became Mesut Özil and, when he was fit, Santi Carzola.

There was clearly a shift in world football which was highlighted by Barcelona in the era of Andres Iniesta and Xavi when suddenly the fashion was to play quick, passing, skilful and technical football. The former manager at the Nou Camp, Pep Guardiola, has even gone so far as to question the worth and value of coaching tackling.

Technically brilliant

But in England, the fact remains that the smaller a player is, the better he has to be technically to succeed. Big, powerful athletes still stand a much better chance even if they are not technically brilliant. That's the difference.

Stoke have signed smaller, technical players. But they kept Ryan Shawcross. When he plays, he's their minder and they win the games. When he doesn't the small, technical players get bullied. They've missed Steven N'Zonzi. Since selling him, they had no presence in midfield. Stoke redressed that by signing Giannelli Imbula for a lot of money. But the Stoke chairman, Peter Coates, justified spending £13m by saying he was young, with good sell-on value and also provided the physical presence they missed since N'Zonzi. That's a modern day transfer right there.

Catching the eye

In fairness, it's the same for any football club, not just Stoke City, a club which can be perceived to be rather touchy when people talk about their reliance on physique, stature and big powerful players.

Per Mertesacker was not at Arsenal because of his technical ability. He was signed and picked because he's a big guy, 6ft 7in, powerful in the air and a big presence. Laurent Koscielny is the same. While he might not be as big as Mertesacker, the Frenchman is not really a technical player – his game is based more on athleticism and power.

Javier Mascherano is 5ft 8in. He played centre half for Barcelona. Could he do that in England every week? No chance. One player who can is Daley Blind because he is an excellent reader of the game and that means, even though he's not overly physical, he can play centre half.

The smaller, but perfectly formed, Javier Mascherano.
(Shutterstock)

Mascherano is the exception to the rule, a short centre half. Players are often picked to play positions based on their size and physical stature. Those sort of decisions come from a young age for players. Small, fast ones are wingers. Big, tall lads are defenders.

But for most of the younger players trying to make it into a first team, they need that physicality and strength. It is also about catching the eye, making a statement and marking themselves down as one to watch for the future.

Wayne Rooney emerged at 16. He was well known in the circles of talent spotting and recruitment – David Pleat had flagged him up from an early age. But the wider world took notice of him when he scored a spectacular goal in the FA Youth Cup. He hit a free kick against the wall, the ball came back and he smashed it into the top corner. Everyone was blown away and the goal was shown everywhere.

He had well and truly caught the eye. But what worked in his favour was that he was physically mature at 16. He had a man's body from a very young age. But the mental side is also very important. A player has got to be mature and psychologically strong to play men's

football. That again, works against the narrow nature of current under-21s football and shows why ending the emergency loan system is a negative step because it will limit the opportunities and flexibility for young players to benefit from an environment that fosters the physical and mental development to be able to play at a senior level.

Boys to men

There are many examples of players going from the Premier League into the Championship and League One clubs to develop their game and even their personality. It's where they grow up and become men. They might even make their debut at a smaller club to come back and make the grade at a big club.

As we have seen, the emergency loan system enabled clubs to loan out and sign players outside of the traditional transfer windows. That system has ended but clubs can still loan players during transfer windows and there is an argument they will now be better prepared and have better planning for the players within both the loaning club and the club taking the player on loan. That could be a positive thing.

But it could stop the flow of players. If an opportunity crops up due to an injury for example, a potential loan deal cannot now be set up. That is bad news because it can limit a player's opportunities for development.

Every manager you speak to will say: 'I want my player out on loan. I want him to become a man.'

End of the fairy tale

With the development of a young player, once he's crossed that white line, made that dream debut, and got into the first team, reality bites – and bites hard. If he is not already at a top club, then everyone is looking to get him to a top club. It's the law of the jungle. Forget the fairy tale: the agent gets straight on the phone to alert scouts and managers to come down to watch your player and get him a big move.

The chief executives and managers of the bigger clubs will be looking. They want the top players. The players know it too, and of course it can affect them. But most of the time they are aware their name is being punted and they enjoy it. Confidence and belief is everything. It puts them in the spotlight – if they're given a chance then they can really progress.

Dele Alli was bought from MK Dons by Tottenham. Their manager Mauricio Pochettino put his arm round Alli and said: 'I believe in you, go and prove me right.' It must have made Alli feel 10 feet tall. It's down to trust and belief and there are few better managers than Pochettino at giving players a chance and giving them great confidence.

There is also an argument that there is too much pressure on the young players. They get in the first teams in the Premier League and suddenly there's a clamour for them to play for England, to go to the World Cup. They are built up into instant superstars, their names are linked in the

papers with bigger clubs because they can earn so much more elsewhere.

There will always be a club – a Manchester City or United, whoever – who can come in and pay more. If Tottenham carry on progressing then suddenly they can pay a bit more. But at the moment if a Tottenham player comes through then those players are liable to be poached by bigger clubs who will pay more money, like Manchester City. That is how it works: it is the football food chain in action.

Perils and pitfalls

As soon as players make their debuts, they are seized upon. They become the next big thing, splashed across the back pages. The press play their part in the hype and building up of young players too soon. Some of the players will handle it, some won't. It depends on their personalities.

But making a debut, being billed as the next wonder kid, being talked about as a future England star suddenly puts players in the spotlight. Some will revel in it and love the attention, even if that attention causes them to focus and go off the rails.

Others will simply not be able to handle it. They might be shy, or say the wrong thing and find it all a bit daunting and a bit overwhelming. They can't handle this attention all of a sudden.

A lot of that comes down to flaws in our clubs and the way we educate our youngsters. At 16, they still have to go to school. After an hour of lessons, they couldn't care less. They don't want to be there, they just want to play football and become a professional footballer. That's their dream now.

From 16, they should be getting media training. It helps them and ensures they can handle the spotlight or media in the future. Some clubs will claim they give media training, putting them in front of a journalist or doing a mocked-up press conference. But if some of these youngsters are going to be thrust into the spotlight, surely they should get more training so then they can handle the focus or the stories that will inevitably arise. But, instead, they are put in at the deep end, many have had too little or no PR training and all of a sudden they are on the front pages, the back pages and leading the rolling sports news bulletin. They cannot handle it.

They are pictured in nightclubs or smoking. If they had had better training, they might have decided to go inside for a cigarette, outside of the public eye and away from cameras. There is a lack of common sense here. If they haven't got great common sense then they need a bit of help.

It will not make anyone a better or worse person by helping them with the media, but it will give them the confidence for their first interview. They can stand up, come across well and not put their foot in it or cause a row.

HITTING THE BIG TIME

Here is a great story – and it is absolutely true. A few years ago, a club was promoted to the Premier League. After the final whistle at the end of the last home game that season, the players came back into the dressing room and hanging on every peg in the dressing room was a rucksack. Each rucksack was filled with cash. Now there's a nice, unexpected bonus. The chairman of the club is incredibly wealthy. He had bankrolled it to the top. It had been a lifelong dream fulfilled and he wanted to say thanks outside of the bonuses written into the contracts, away from the taxman. The players, naturally, absolutely loved it. No names, no questions, all top secret. And all completely against the rules, of course.

Breaking all the rules

There are strict rules imposed by the Premier League and Football League that bonuses – for promotions, wins, points tallies, and other clauses – must be written into contracts and agreed by a certain date at the start of each season.

Otherwise, bonuses would be cropping up left, right and centre, not to say the prospect of illegal incentives to beat teams and win games. It opens up the whole system to potential abuse.

But the Premier League do not do anything about players going on holiday, which, if the circumstances are right, can be classed as a bonus.

Cast adrift

If club owners treat players to an expensive foreign trip, that is some bonus. There is a great story from one top club where the players were given a surprise holiday at the end of a particular season. They went to stay on the owner's yacht which was moored in some exotic location and one of the players, who likes a beer or 10, went up to the owner and, in his drunken state, told him he was not showing enough ambition, should spend more, and who he should buy.

Good luck with that one. Because the first thing the owner did after the holiday was tell the manager that the offending player was being sold.

Million pound men

Football, as has been clearly established, is all about money. And people would be naïve to think it was all above board and the taxman – let alone the football authorities – knew about all the money going into people's pockets.

One club allegedly promised players £1m-per-man if they won a trophy. They didn't, of course. But did it give them extra energy, legs and incentives in certain games? Probably. Is it fair? Well, that depends on the Premier League's strict bonus rules and whether the bonuses were declared and above board. Probably not.

The trappings of success. If you have the money, flaunt it – and most do. (Shutterstock)

Some owners, chief executives or chairmen have got more money than sense.

One owner of a club was not interested in squabbling or negotiations in one particular deal. He was signing the son of a friend of his. All the owner kept saying was: 'Just get it done. I don't care – just get it done.' Money is not an issue when it come to friends. And if their football clubs allow them to do a friend a favour then money really is no object. He was a good young player, the owner wanted him and could do his friend a favour. It was a win-win.

Easy life, easy money

Here's another story that everyone in the game knows about. It concerns a much-travelled striker who has made no secret of the fact in dressing rooms up and down the country that he's in it purely for the money.

He had the chance to sign for one club – a bigger club with loftier ambitions, but didn't fancy it because another club was closer to where he lived. He could not be bothered with the commute. Both clubs were paying the same, it was an absolute no-brainer. The striker was purely driven by money rather than any ambitions on the pitch and fancied an easier life with no commuting as an added bonus.

For some players, of course, it is all about the money. Many people outside of the game have long suspected that, and those of us on the inside can confirm it is true. No one should be in any doubt about that. Some still want to be successful,

win trophies, but for all of them, as ever, it's always about one-upmanship when it comes to certain things.

'I've got more money than you, I earn more than you, I've got better boots, I've slept with more women than you, got more cars than you.' Whatever it might be, nothing is off limits. All the time they are bragging about how much they earn, how much they get in bonuses, and how much better their contract is.

••• WHAT THE AGENT SAID

An alternative reality

Football is a completely different world to what the general public are used to. Players live on a different planet. They receive so much criticism for their wealth and lavish lifestyles. It is to many eyes ridiculous what they earn. They are thrust from obscurity into stardom and wealth. But if the general public earned as much then they would do the same as well: the spending would get out of hand and they would be showing off their cars, their wealth and their fame and fortune.

But if players want to go and waste their money on an extraordinarily expensive car or holiday, then let them do it. It is not their fault that they get paid so much. It's the business they are in. Actors, for example, do not get this sort of criticism. Bankers and stockbrokers get a bit of it because they are often wealthy and indulgent. But you never see it with actors, musicians and others. If they go out on a bender, earn too much and get crazy money, then no-one slags them off for it. Why not? It's still showbiz. Is it because more people in this country are jealous of footballers than young movie stars? It must be something because footballers are treated very differently.

The shallow end

A player of seven or eight years of age does not sign up to be a role model. They sign up to be a footballer. Aspiring players when they are a bit older are not earning crazy money then and are probably not thinking about it until later in life when the money and earnings kick in. Up to that point, players just want to be players.

Some footballers are not the sharpest tools in the box. At 14 to 16, for them it's all about boots. But, if they are that shallow, if that's all they're worried about – not who is the best agent for them but who can get them the best or most fashionable boots of the day – then they are probably not worried about their long-term prospects, development or what is best for them.

Tattoo you

The players all know each other and football is their life, on and off the pitch. They lose touch with their old lives, their old school mates and it's all about teammates and what they are doing.

It's all about trends. If one player gets a watch or a car, the rest of the dressing room get them. It's the same with tattoos. Ten years ago there weren't many tattoos to be seen in football. David Beckham in all probability kicked it off because he's covered in them and he started the fashion. Now they are all covered in tattoos. One day some player will stop having them and the rest of them will follow like sheep and tattoos will be out of fashion all of a sudden.

They've all got the same haircut. A favourite is having it shaved and then long on top. One big player starts it and they all follow.

It's the same with boots. One player wears certain boots and they all follow

Neymar of Brazil
and his haircut
from the 2014
World Cup.
(Shutterstock)

David Beckham
showing that his
creativity knows no
bounds, especially
when it comes to
tattoos! (Getty)

suit. It is a unique world, not because of young men copying each other, as happens in all walks of life, but because of the financial means to copy and compete. It is a different mindset people find fascinating and why the general public want a glimpse into the lifestyle of football and footballers.

Then as the player grows up, it changes from boots to even more expensive boys' toys. From 18 to 20 it's all about cars, then it becomes watches, and then houses as they become older and older.

Supercars for superstars

Dressing rooms are brutal. They can also be unforgiving places in which there can be some appalling behaviour. This can be sexist, racist, and often bullying in nature. The mentality is all about finding a weakness, engaging in one-upmanship, and competing to be 'better'.

If one player walks in with a £4,000 Rolex, the guy next to him will want one worth six grand. If one player buys a new Ferrari California, then his teammate is going to get a new Bugatti Veyron.

But if anyone thinks this all stops with the playground-style bragging at youth level then they are very much mistaken. It goes right the way to the top into the international dressing rooms. It's why so much player unrest can follow players going away on international duty.

There will be a player in that dressing room bragging that he earns £200,000-a-week (he probably doesn't). That will make other players resentful. One might go back to his club complaining that he only gets £125,000-a-week.

Then the next time the squad gets together the '£200k' player will approach the resentful teammate saying that his club manager has had a word, and asking if he wants to meet? Because if he signs, then, naturally, he'll earn £200,000-a-week.

Country club

International get-togethers, whereby club players called up for international duty go to training camps, are lethal in regard of player unrest because of the bragging and one-upmanship that goes on. The agents bear much of the brunt of the ensuing unrest as well.

The Swedish national team training and most likely swapping bragging rights. (Getty)

Ego building

Now the FA are getting in on the act by building up the players and their egos. They are saying the England players are going to win the World Cup in 2022.

Going away with England or whichever international team is rife with tapping-up. Chelsea players will tap up Liverpool players and vice versa. It happens everywhere. When Cesc Fabregas was on international duty with Spain, they were putting Barcelona shirts on him even though he was then an Arsenal player. It was completely out of hand. But it

happened and in a very blatant way.

Tapping up in football goes on every day. Right now, one household name footballer is being tapped up because it happens every moment of every day.

When we talk about tapping up, it's coming from every angle. That is absolutely guaranteed. Whatever it might be, for another agent, for another club, for a boot company, it goes on all the time. Rumours often get out. And when a big story breaks in the national press – like Ashley Cole meeting Chelsea in secret behind Arsenal's back, for which he and Chelsea were both fined – it ends up on every back page.

Negotiations over the breakfast buffet

One player, a really big name, before the 2014 World Cup, was unsettled and fancied a move. He had gone stale with his club at the time. He met with two other big clubs at the England team hotel. One club was represented by their manager, the other by a chief executive.

At the tournament itself, a big name manager was out there for the whole duration. He met with his big summer signing, the player's agent and got the deal done.

He nearly signed another player when – surprise, surprise – he just happened to be having breakfast in the hotel at the same time as the mother of the second player. Negotiations were done over the breakfast buffet. Unfortunately, the muesli can't have been good enough, because the player went to another club.

24-hour tapping up

Tapping up comes from every angle of the game. Managers get tapped up for other managerial jobs, for example. It's the reason why as soon as a player features in the first team, his name appears in the paper in some form or other, and he is being linked with a big move.

One Football League chairman complained recently: 'Our player has been tapped up.' The previous day that same chairman had rung another player to try and sign him to replace his player that had been tapped up.

It can become a little bit irritating with the clubs. If they don't want a player, that football club will be on the phone to every other club, agent or chief executive trying to get rid of the player. He's for sale, they want to do a deal and often they'll offer to pay some of the player's wages. That's how it works. One minute, you're flavour of the month, the next you're being pushed out of the door. The double standards are incredible. They moan one day about tapping up, the next day they are trying to flog players to all and sundry.

Danny Higginbotham, the former Stoke player, gave a fascinating insight on talkSPORT. He was saying he had been on pre-season, didn't want to leave Stoke, and turned a move down to stay at the Britannia Stadium. Next thing he

⟨•••⟩ WHAT THE AGENT SAID

Go now – or never play again

In 2011, Peter Crouch was at Tottenham and the club's owner Daniel Levy wanted to sell him. Levy wanted to cash in promptly; the player did not want to sign a new contract, and Levy would never let contracts run down because it devalues the asset even if he wanted to sell, but Crouch was in no hurry to leave.

Levy made it very clear that if Crouch did not agree to leave, he would not be included in Tottenham's Premier League squad. This was not an idle threat. It was very real. An England player was being told he would be left to rot because the club wanted to sell him. Sure enough, Crouch went to Stoke on deadline day for £12m. Levy is a brilliant negotiator, hard as nails and there's no room for sentiment.

All this talk about players being disloyal, greedy and pushing for moves has to be put into context because it happens the other way all of the time. If a football club does not want a player then they will flog him without a second thought. If a football club wants a player, they will tap him up. Similarly, if an agent does not want a player then the agent will dump him to tap up the next client, and vice versa. Tapping up goes on all of the time. It's rife in every aspect of the game. And it's so easy as well.

knew he was flying in economy class while the rest of the squad were in business class. That's how clubs treat players when they don't want them anymore. And Stoke are pretty good with players. Their chairman Peter Coates couldn't be more honourable.

The tapping up of players is ridiculous. There's no doubt in any agent's mind that players are tapped up every day. How often in every single day just depends on how good the players concerned are, how close they are to a move. There are always rumours about players. One young player got rid of or 'knocked' his agent just before a move. His uncle actually did the deal, pocketed the cash and the agency who had until recently represented the player and done much of the negotiation, did not get a penny. Yet still they put out a tweet congratulating the player on the move so as not to lose face. That's how crazy football is and how it works. It's a crazy world.

Contacts are king

For tapping up to happen, contact has to be made. Usually that's an initial phone call. The harder part of getting phone numbers is when players are younger. It can be hard if they're an unknown teenager. If they are a big star, someone an agent knows will have their number and pass it on. Other players, scouts, clubs or even journalists. Someone has always got a number. Next thing you know, a player is getting a call and it's someone saying: 'Do you fancy this move?'

Know who is know how

Agents have to be careful about dealing with relatives, as those relations can get ideas in their heads and become agents themselves. The business is all about contacts and who you know and what you know. Some relatives can be at an advantage in that regard. There are dads who know everybody in the game from being on the touchline, watching their kids week in and week out.

But not many really know many in the game. They might know the manager, chairman and owner at their player's club, but not much beyond that in the wider game. Most would not know how to draw up a contract, bonuses, signing-on fee and so on. They would be in serious danger of selling their son, brother, nephew or whoever, short.

Tapping up can start with a scout having a chat to an agent, saying the manager of a club likes a player, and that he is going in for a meeting with the chief scout to discuss future plans. The chief scout drops into conversation: 'I like Player X, he looks a good player.' The agent will suddenly claim that he knows the player, can get him and next thing you know there's an agent trying to tap up the player to get the deal done.

There will be whispers, tapping up and the wheels are set in motion. One player might tap up another, a phone call made and suddenly it's happening.

Astronomical money is an open secret

It's very rare to get a phone call out of the blue these days to tell you that a club is going in to sign a player. A good agent knows that in advance in any case. The problem is lots of other agents know about the signing as well. They will get busy. They'll gossip, hear something and get on the phone offering to do a deal, and help

get players to sign for clubs.

Everyone will know what the club are willing to pay to get the player. It is an open secret. Chelsea were offering £50,000-a-week for a reserve keeper not so long ago. John Stones was being offered a huge contract in the summer of 2015, a big signing-on fee and loyalty bonuses. They were huge amounts of money on offer.

It was a surprise that Everton did not sell John Stones earlier than they did. Most people in football thought they'd cash in but they held firm until they received a whopping £47.5m from Manchester City. It paid off but sometimes it is hard to know what a club stands to gain from holding firm. They look stronger, defiant and yet it's a gamble because if they end up selling for less or being made to look silly next time around, what have they gained? Nothing.

Jumping tall, former Spurs player Peter Crouch. (Shutterstock)

Football agents have their work cut out for them dealing with clients. (Shutterstock)

09

THE PITFALLS

Once a player gets into the first team then it's all about what goes on in his head. Does he have the mental strength to tough it out and stay in the first team? And that's not really a question concerning sporting ability: there are so many trappings on and off the pitch, and suddenly, a young man goes from being a virtual unknown to being a famous celebrity. It can be a dangerous time. Players not only need to keep their heads but also to be able to rely on everyone around them. Otherwise it is all too easy to go off the rails, lose your head, and get carried away with your own hype.

'What can you get me?'

This is the period when a player needs his friends, family and a good agent to protect him the most. Some players will listen, some players won't. Most players view an agent as a bit of a leech. But a good agent will support his client, appreciating that the job is far from finished. Players think about it or even appreciate and understand when people are trying to guide them in the right way. It's all about what their agent can get them. How much is it worth? What's the deal worth? New contract, new boot deal and the next big advertising deal. It is a selfish market.

Sticking together like glue – many players tend to stick to friends of their own kind. (Shutterstock)

Following the crowd

There is a widely held view in football that most players are thick. They're not thinking beyond the next pay cheque. Go back to the early days when they're kids and it's all about boots. As they get older then it's cars, watches and houses. Footballers have a craving for the same stuff. They drive the same car, all wear the same clothes, all have the same headphones, wear similar watches. It's like a uniform.

Most players are not individuals really. When players leave school and go into a football environment, not many hold onto those old school friends. Not many players, when they're 25, still have that old school network of friends draped round them when they're midway into their careers. See them on a night out and it's likely to be with other footballers, not old school friends.

Unfortunately, there's a level of jealousy with the old school friends. The average Joe is jealous that his mate is earning £100,000-a-week and he's working his proverbials off in an office for £40,000-a-year. That's life and why footballers go their own way and hang out together.

Social scene

Most footballers have one mate – possibly two – from back in the day but the majority of the people they are friends with are other footballers because, inevitably, they all get to know each other in what is an exclusive environment. They all live in that little footballers' bubble. They take a step out of reality, live in a goldfish bowl and not many players, by the time they are 23, 24 or 25, have many friends from school. They're all footballers.

Also, socialising is different. Players cannot go out on a Thursday or Friday night because there is a game on Saturday. When a player's old school friends are going out, having big weekends, the players are early to bed, staying in, and getting ready for the game.

But on a night when there is not a game in the next day or two, go to a nightclub in London and the footballers are all hanging out together because they're out while their old school mates are staying in because they have to get up for their 9-to-5 work the next morning.

Football is a close-knit business. Speak to a player at Bristol City, ask him about someone at Middlesbrough and he'll know him, from when they had a night out together not so long ago. Football is like one big bubble. Everyone knows each other, they hang out together, play against each other and it's like one big social club.

Playboy players

A player's life is not reality – it is far removed from it. Most players are detached from the real world. Most outsiders have it in their heads that footballers will leave school at 16, go full time, get into the first team but still be friends with their school mates. But once they are in the professional world, those old bonds break down very quickly. That is the reality.

The temptation when a player first breaks in and starts earning the big money, is to indulge himself. He'll want to go out and buy a Prada suit, date three Miss Worlds and get drunk on champagne every night.

A player must at least try to stay grounded. But a lot of them do go off the rails.

If you're a player then suddenly you get into nightclubs for free, you get your drinks for free. Your mere presence is enough, and the owners will put up pictures of you on their website, simply to show off who's been in their nightclub.

There are all sorts of temptations, and, of course, women are a major one. Traditionally, managers liked their players to marry young and settle down – or at least give the impression of domestic bliss. The reality, especially in the modern game, is that every day of the week, players are being tempted. It is a sad fact of football life that girls throw themselves at footballers. There are still kiss-and-tells as much as the WAGs who just want a footballer as a boyfriend, or the genuine love stories.

Spend, spend, spend

Pitfalls also lie in wait for the player who takes his foot off the gas because there is always someone ready to take his place. The competition is far greater now,

and that is why, while the whole nightclub scene is still thriving, it has diminished because footballers realise there is someone there ready to come and take their place if they slip up.

But players are more hungry than ever for the money. Some just want to spend, spend, spend.

There are some players who leave it up to their agents to control their bank accounts because they cannot stop spending money. They clear £40,000-a-month and yet, by the end of the month, they can be overdrawn every single time.

Modern football is littered with stories of players who have lost their fortunes,

Player power – Arsenal teammates hanging out at work and at play. (Getty)

The first 'playboy' footballer George Best. (Getty)

often due to gambling addictions. Matt Etherington and Michael Chopra are both prime examples but it is a bigger, wider problem. Players get on their phones, either to make a call or on a bookies' app, and suddenly they are putting £5,000 on horse racing, boxing, American football or whatever it is possible to bet on.

Players love to gamble on golf when they are playing against each other. There's so many pitfalls when it comes to gambling. Footballers love a buzz, and the prospect of betting huge sums provides a major thrill.

Gangster's paradise

It is incredible the number of players who end up hanging around with organised criminals. The gangsters are always in the same nightclubs. The criminals love having footballers as their mates and the footballers enjoy hanging around with gangsters and becoming wannabe gangsters themselves.

There's stories of one big player being threatened by the local gangsters. They made him stay, they wouldn't let him leave.

Spitting angry

I've seen players being spat at in the street, and that's not an uncommon occurrence.

There's an awful story where a player was having dinner with his wife in a nice restaurant. A man came over and spat in his food. Apparently the player's team had lost that day, and fans do not like to

see players out and about after a defeat. It appears that some man thought that entitled him to be able to spit in another person's dinner.

It is disgusting behaviour which no one should have to put up with. It is understandable that players should be sensible and cannot be seen out enjoying themselves after a defeat. But people don't know what players – and their families – have to put up with. I've heard people in the pub trying to justify it. But there is absolutely no justification.

Easy targets

Footballers are a target. Often players are picked on for no reason other than they are a well-known footballer. That's why players like protection and being

WHAT THE AGENT SAID

'Wrong 'uns'

It's strange how many players know characters of criminal and downright dangerous repute – in slang terms, complete and utter 'wrong 'uns'. Players can go from knowing a few faces, seeing them at games week-in and week-out. Then suddenly the top geezers are suddenly socialising with other players in the team. As an agent I knew who they were, but suddenly other players had become big mates with them. It's weird. It's all about status. And it's about status for both parties. They love it.

Some players like having gangsters around, someone to look after them. There's talk of one Premier League player actually being a member of a gang. When he's out, the boss of the gang, the main man, is out with the player. He's out wherever he goes.

There's talk of a lot of players getting mugged for their watches, having them nicked in a club. There's talk someone got stabbed on a night out. But nothing was ever reported to the police. Why? Because the gangsters all took care of it.

There's some proper wrong 'uns out there. Horrible pieces of work.

There have been many stories about players stealing from their colleagues out of dressing rooms, going through teammates' lockers and stealing things like watches and jewellery. There is one young player who got caught and was immediately sacked.

looked after. That's why they befriend the hardmen, the local gangsters. Players can be in bars, being completely innocent, and doing nothing wrong. Sitting at tables, sipping glasses of champagne. There's nothing wrong with that. But that will not stop drunken idiots coming up to them and saying: 'You're a tosser, you're too flash.'

It's really nasty. Most players will turn their back. They'll ask them politely to stop, saying 'Leave me alone, mate. I'm out with friends.' But sometimes that is not enough and they need someone else to be blunter. That's why they'll have a

couple of people around them who can tell the pests to f*** off. I've even done it myself – stood up and said: 'F*** off, he's out with his friends, leave him alone.'

Success and failure

There's a fine line between success and failure. It partly explains why footballers are misunderstood. Players are always on that edge between success and failure. People argue how can Wayne Rooney be under pressure because he's earned £200,000-a-week for the last five years.

But no one can think Wayne Rooney wants to go home, be bombed by Manchester United, be seen as a failure by his kids? No chance. He might earn that money and be a multi-millionaire, but he still wants to be a success. He still wants to win trophies and I think there's an added pressure to the footballer in that success and failure issue. Even as his career at Old Trafford ended, Rooney was driven by a determination to carry on playing, fulfil his boyhood dream of returning to Everton and help them be successful again.

It is the same whether a player is in the Championship, Champions League or League Two. No-one wants to be relegated. Players want to be successful and they're always teetering on the brink of success and failure.

That's does not excuse some of the behaviour that arises with footballers. But it is a fact of life. There's so much pressure. People think the money compensates fully for it. But the money does not make up for everything a player has to go through and experience.

That is another reason why players always hang around with other players. It's their comfort zone. Their safety net.

Enjoying each other's company and sharing a selfie, Neymar (left) and Claudio Bravo. (Getty)

If residing in the Championship – clubs like QPR can still provide a decent level of income for a good player. (Shutterstock)

Big club, little talent

Players have also got to behave well off the pitch otherwise their game suffers and careers decline very quickly. It is not purely about living well, but talent as well. Or, more to the point, lack of talent or being hyped far too much.

There is one player who broke into the first team at a club, got into the England squad, landed a big-money move and signed a contract for £50,000-a-week in an overall £15m deal. Yet he completely failed – 'bombed'.

The reason is because he is at heart a decent Championship player. He had found his level, it didn't work out at the big club and he went back to where he started. It is to his credit that he got his career going again. And in the meantime he earned a lot of money, and two of his brothers got jobs.

He's such a typical example. He could be in the wilderness because it all went

wrong so quickly. He went to the big club, liked the social life a bit too much but saw sense and worked hard to get his career back on track.

All aboard the gravy train

Once a player hits the Premier League, he generally stays there. Even if his club goes down, there is generally someone else ready to buy him. It's because clubs like to buy players who have Premier League experience.

There are a lot of players in the Premier League squads who make a series of moves but never stay long at any one club and don't exactly set the world on fire. It leaves fans thinking, 'How the hell are you still in the Premier League?'

Before parachute payments were

introduced, whereby relegated clubs received payment from the Premier League in subsequent seasons to cushion the financial blow, players would be desperate to leave the relegated club. Relegation could see them take a big drop in wages, particularly if there were relegation clauses in their contract. Now players don't care so much about leaving and getting back into the Premier League because they're still earning big money in the Championship.

The Premier League is a merry-go-round in which talent happily gets on and off riding different horses each time. While there is a massive financial gap between the Premier and the Football leagues, wealth is actually dripping down into the Championship now because the clubs in that division used to pay £5,000-a-week. Now they are paying £20,000-a-week, and a lot of that is due to the parachute money.

Championship status, elite money

The Championship is by far and away on a different level to any other country's second tier. None of Italy, Spain, or Germany are generating anything like the money which English and Welsh Championship clubs pay out in terms of contracts or transfer fees. Players at that level can suddenly find themselves famous, rich and never having to think about working again.

Looked after

There's players who are 18, they befriend the first team players, get on with them and the first teamers like it as well. The big players will speak to them, take them under their wing. You might see it as strange because they're 18-year-olds

going around with 28-year-olds. But the point is they're all footballers, they don't care. There's no ageism. They're just footballers. It's just how the whole circle works – get in with the 'in crowd' and you are made at that football club.

There's one young lad who was 17. For some reason another player, 10 years older, took the kid under his wing. He's got signed shirts, stuff he bought him, he liked him, he's his little man. He used to pick him up and drive him to training and all that. He really liked that. The kid befriended him, got involved in first team training, did well and suddenly the player became big mates with him. They liked the same stuff, they mixed together and the older player would give him his old stuff like TVs, his old gear, anything and everything really. He just looked out for him. He'd take him on nights out. If he was going to Nando's, he'd ring him, take him and he'd always pay. He'd always look after him.

He was on nothing. Very low money. The other player was on £30,000-a-week so he'd pay for him. His agent would ring up the kid and say: 'Where are you?' He'd reply and say: 'I'm in Nando's with him.' What are you doing with him again? It's a bit weird. He'd take him on first team days out, he'd pay for him and it's a million miles away from reality.

The old days are long gone

The days of apprentices cleaning boots don't exist anymore. Time has moved on.

The initiation ceremonies – where youngsters or new signings have to do something to bond themselves into the new squad – still go on and they are very good. The young kids will probably have to stand up after training or on the coach for an away game and sing a song to the first team. All the older, big signings have to do it as well. It's tradition, it's part of the culture. It's great that it still happens. It's important that there's still a bit of fun.

Other habits, however, have changed. Players still go out and eat or drink to excess but the young ones today are a lot healthier than previous generations. Clubs are careful about what they serve in the canteen, because great stress is placed on the importance of a healthy diet.

Players today recognise that because of the money involved now, they have to do anything they can – whatever it takes – to make it. If that means not drinking then so be it. Many players are teetotal. They watch everything they eat. Chicken, fish, boiled vegetables. Most players do understand and eat well. It can make all the difference – as can the smallest of treats. At the Football Association's training HQ at St George's Park there's a

Starbucks within the complex but Gareth Southgate introduced a rule to remove all the sweet treats from the counter so players would not be tempted by a piece of chocolate to go with their cappuccino – that's how important every piece of food is for a footballer.

Too much too young

The problem is that if a players lands the big-money deal too quickly then it takes out the hunger to get into the first team. If you're a millionaire, what's the incentive to get into the first team? To earn more money, naturally. But there's a fine line between chasing the money and getting too much too soon.

A lot of people think you should only get the big money if you've reached the top. There's so many analysts out of the City running our football clubs. Look at Brentford – they introduced a system to

pick a player. They don't have people out there watching games, they've got people watching stats. They've taken out the human element. You've got to sign the player because of what he can do on the pitch and as a player. Not just sign him because he's 6ft 3in, 12 stone and has made lots of interceptions. A player can be identified on a laptop rather than by an old-school scout standing on the touchline. At Fulham, there have been strict rules about a player fitting into age categories, having a sell-on value and it is all based on *Moneyball* – every player must be seen as a financial asset.

The emphasis on the EPPP is to get all of the best young players in category one clubs so they're actually making it easy for the big clubs to nick the best young players. Is that right? No, probably not. It's not right because if football sets out to encourage the best young players to

The Manchester City training ground has amongst its facilities a canteen, where the players can relax and have a balanced diet. (Getty)

go to the best academies then what is the point of smaller clubs then breeding good players for the future?

Sometimes you get too many good players in one place. You can come out of that place, step down a level and play first team football and become better.

One Championship manager says the best way to educate his young players is to send them to Scotland, join a small club, get lumps kicked out of him for three months, live in a terrible one-bedroom flat with mice and rats – and turn him into a man. Then he'll be ready.

Born with a silver spoon

In football, as in life in general, there exists the syndrome whereby some players are born with a silver spoon in their mouth. For a young player at Chelsea, he is surrounded by world-class footballers in the senior squad, benefits from wonderful facilities, and the club can sign all the best young talent because of the way the EPPP system is organised. However, it creates a bottleneck of aspiring players trying to get through.

Many are sent out on loan and that brings a change to their lifestyle. They might still have the money, but the environment is often very different, especially outside London because the capital is often about bright lights and glamour. You go from one of the big London clubs with all the trappings of a big city to a small provincial town and it's

a big culture shock. It brings players down to earth with a bump. And that's a good thing. It helps with the development of young players to be sent out, play some loan football, get lumps kicked out of him, have to live in a less than luxurious flat and see a little bit of how the real world works. They soon grow up then.

Easy, easy?

It's good for people outside the game to understand how difficult it can be to be a footballer. The average Joe thinks being a footballer is easy. It really is not. Players are paid very well, but the statistics show how hard it is to break through. Not many players, whatever club they are at, break

into the first team and stay there. To keep trying, to keep working hard requires considerable strength of character. If a player is mentally strong enough, and wants it enough, then it will help him get over that difficult period early in his career when he is struggling to make the breakthrough.

Good money after bad

There are huge pitfalls. There are agents leading players up the garden path, financial advisers selling get-rich-quick schemes, cajoling players to invest in all sorts of ventures from bonds to restaurants, nightclubs to shares.

Things can go bad. Seriously bad. West Ham players were taken in by a hamper

It's one thing signing for a big club, it's another breaking through into the first team. (Getty)

scam in 2014. They paid thousands for hampers that never materialised and the offender was found guilty of fraud. That showed that no matter how wealthy footballers are, they still love a bargain even if it's something they don't really need. The 'investments' fool players time and again.

A national obsession

When England play, particularly in the European Championships or the World Cup, the whole country shuts down to watch it. Matches are played in the afternoons in tournaments, and the country will come to a complete standstill. Everyone will be knocking off work, offices will have TVs in them, and it will bring the nation to a halt.

And that proves it: football has become show business, appealing to a much more diverse audience.

In Mexico and the World Cup in 1986, England played games against Poland when they had to win. But the whole country did not come to a standstill then. Not everyone was obsessed with football like they are now. Even in 1997 when England drew 0-0 with Italy in Rome and therefore qualified for the World Cup the next year, the fevered attention wasn't on the same scale as it is today.

Once upon a time the football audience was dominated by male, 18-to 45-year-olds. That was the demographic of the football fan.

But watching England against Ecuador in 2006 for the World Cup in Stuttgart, the main square was full of a wide variety of England fans. Perhaps half of the fans there were families, women and children and they were there to watch England play football. The transition among England fans – and football fans generally – is incredible.

Hard to handle

But with that growing popularity comes increasing demands. The question is are footballers really made to handle it?

Young players get into the game primarily because they love football. That comes before the money and anything else. A kid watches his football team as he grows up, dreaming of being the player on the pitch, scoring the winner at Old Trafford, Arsenal or wherever.

The reality of what happens if that dream comes true is very different. Is there enough training (both on and off the pitch) for young players to be able to fully handle it? Some players who drop out of the game will feel football clubs fail them. They say there's no-one to really explain the pitfalls, the dangers and the celebrity of the game. There's no-one there to say if you play for England then you can bring a nation to a standstill, end up on the front page as a hero or a villain after a football match. The pressure is huge.

Look at what happened to David Beckham after France 98. Effigies of him were hung from lampposts because he got sent off. That's the price of fame and not football.

Becoming a role model

The concept of role model and the relationship to footballers is a fascinating one. One argument is that footballers are role models whether they like it or not. But if that is the case, it is only right that they must be taught and guided to teach them what that means, how they must behave and what they have to do.

The sport is littered with examples. One recently concerns Jack Grealish at Aston Villa, who has received widespread

💬 WHAT THE AGENT SAID

Front page fags

Jack Wilshere smoking a cigarette in Las Vegas should not really worry anyone – until you realise footballers are now celebrities and it makes front page news. Why? Because it's showbiz. But he's not. He's a footballer, this is the guy who just kicks the ball around a park. Footballers shouldn't be role models but the reality is that he is a role model, whether he likes it or not. And surely that's not right. Is an actor in *EastEnders* a role model? They have a fag, why aren't they on the front page? That's the point.

There will be people on this planet who don't play football but they have a fag. But, because he's a footballer, it's seen as a sport, it's seen as a fitness thing, he can't have a fag, but it's hard to believe – and a few of us will smoke occasionally – that the odd cigarette will really hurt you. There's not one written thing, or scientific proof that will really prove that it will make you a worse footballer. It's impossible to believe one cigarette, once in a blue moon, will make you a worse footballer, so why is it a story? But it ends up on the front page.

It's hard to understand a newspaper editor who sits there, decides what's going on the front page and says: 'I'll tell you what we're going to run with, Jack Wilshere is having a fag in Las Vegas, that's going to be on the front page.' It's showbiz, front page, it's football. If we go back to that day when Jack Wilshere made front page news for smoking and look up what was happening in the world, then I don't believe that there wasn't a more important news story. But it's showbiz and that's the point. The life cycle of a footballer is no longer about just being a footballer. It's now also about being a showbiz personality. Every human being is now judging you on that. They are judging you on everything you do. You didn't sign up to that when you signed a contract at 16.

It just goes to prove that these days footballers are celebrities. That's why they are on the front page. The players will complain but the reader craves the gossip and probably thinks they should behave themselves, they are well paid and should learn to be a bit better in public.

💬 WHAT THE AGENT SAID

Listen and learn

What is needed is an educational hour a week on what life could be like for a 16-year-old. Even if just 10 per cent get something that makes them think and realise that if they're playing in the Premier League at 18, earning £20,000-a-week, and just been thrashed away from home, and the team is bottom of the league, that it might be a good idea to stay at home that night. Get a few mates round at home, don't go to a nightclub, don't get photographed lying on the floor, drunk. A bit of simple education, some life skills, coping with the showbiz lifestyle could work wonders. Educate them, give them a little bit of help, try and tweak them just a little bit. Tickle their brain, make them think and realise: 'Yeah, I'll stay in that night.'

Here's some advice: don't go on Snapchat, send pictures to your mates of you smoking a bong, because it will be spread around. Or worse, a friend sells it to a newspaper. The amount of players who get caught on social media is astonishing. Teach them not to do it. Get taught by a professional who is away from football.

exposure for his off-the-pitch behaviour and hard partying, with the usual criticism that he is not acting as a role model should.

Some of what Grealish has done, chiefly his partying, is not the smartest thing to do. News reporters picked up on it, and sure enough there were the usual features of 'what's gone wrong with the new generation of footballers?'

Youngsters like Grealish learn the hard way. What should be done is to sit these boys down when they're 16 and talk to them, and in a way they will understand.

Friendly advice from people players trust is more likely to succeed. The game is trying to make up for a lack of education of its young, raw recruits.

At 14, kids are given scholarships. They won't give a damn about school. Parents try to make them, but the kids are too busy thinking about football and their careers as a footballer.

Learn from the pros
What is needed is someone who knows how to educate people in a specific setting. Someone separate from a football club, but someone who still talks in football terms – who talks the players' language. There's a way of educating players and providing practical ways to stay out of trouble. Someone could have told Jack Wilshere how to avoid being photographed in public and also urged him to never be seen smoking a cigarette.

Survive all that...

A top player should be set up for life financially. Wayne Rooney is one such survivor. He has evolved. He's gone from being a footballer with this reputation of being thick to being a diplomat, speaking brilliantly after the Paris attacks. He spoke so well, with so much maturity. Rooney is

Someone who has matured and shown compassion when it mattered is Wayne Rooney. (Shutterstock)

now in his 30s, coming towards the end of his career, and has matured.

Yet no-one prepares players for the end of their careers. Players like Gareth Bale or Wayne Rooney who have gone all the way to the top, are very wealthy and won't be in need of money in retirement. Sadly too many players will do.

What now?
You're still 35, potentially have got 50 more years on the planet, and you want something to do. But what? No-one is preparing you for the next chapter or giving you advice. You've had 15 years of the absolute buzz, the incredible high of being a footballer. That cannot be switched off just like that. That has huge implications for the human being that a footballer is. No-one is preparing you for that. That is a failure of service from everyone in the game.

Jack Grealish (left front) trains hard, possibly working off a hangover? (Getty)

ENEMIES WITHIN

Agents have become intermediaries now. The FA have less control, and there is more scope for people to break the rules because the rules have been relaxed to the point the business is unregulated. It means the industry is sailing close to the wind. The game is plagued by chaos, intimidation and incompetence.

Inhibitions v incentives

As ever, the driving force is money. People see pound signs and they lose their inhibitions. They might question and consider if they really should be acting in the ways they are but the financial incentives are so large it does not stop them.

It was reported in the national press that one of the biggest guys at the Football Association, their financial regulation officer Martin Fauvel, left to go and work for an agent, Will Salthouse.

He would be the guy on the other end of the line when agents would ring up about money coming in, contracts and transfers. He would know all the details.

Now, he's switched sides and he even sent round an e-mail to the agents. 'Hi all. After four fantastic years as a gamekeeper, I am soon to turn poacher. I start a new venture as head of operations for Unique Sports Management.'

Sleep with one eye open

Football will eat itself one day. But the problem is that there is so much wealth on offer, so many millionaires, so many millions to be made, that everyone is trying to turn everyone else over.

There are all sorts of threats to players, agents, managers, directors and chief executives. Everyone in the business has had a conversation that runs along the lines of, 'You don't know who you're dealing with. Watch your back.' It would be a big surprise for an agent, working at a certain level, who had not been threatened.

Agents have been warned: 'I'm going to do you. Sleep with one eye open.' That 'discussion' is very common when one agent is accused of poaching clients. There will be threats of retaliation, with claims an aggrieved agent will steal all of the accused's players. That is an all-too-common occurrence.

Wild West

Some agents deservedly have a bad name but, in contrast, a lot of agents feel that the FA are incompetent. Effectively there are no regulations – no-one is stopping the threats, lies and tapping up. Everyone thinks they can get away with anything. It's like the Wild West.

What happens between agents is not really important in terms of the footballer. In fact, the agent will do everything possible to try and shield the player from all the off-the-field antics, the behind-the-scenes nonsense. But the nasty side of the business is never far away.

WHAT THE AGENT SAID

Sweeteners and backhanders

Footballers should sign with agents in the belief they can do the best job for them. But the reality is players are swayed by sweeteners and backhanders. One agent I know said about 70 per cent of footballers are not totally happy with their agent for one reason or another.

In fact, a lot of footballers go with agents for the wrong reason, be that financial, recommendations or even just on a whim. But it would be a shock if more than 30 per cent were completely happy with their agent.

A lot of players sign for the wrong reasons. And that's where the enemy from within comes into play. Everyone is sniping against each other, trying to make a fast buck out of the latest talent.

Young players will sign for an agent just for a pair of boots. Older players will sign for an agent because they've been given £50,000. Others will sign for the price of a Range Rover. The dressing room banter that goes on when one player starts bragging to another that he's signed with an agent because he's given him a car, given his mate a job or some cash, results in some predictable 'banter'.

It leaves players sitting at home, thinking: 'I haven't got the right agent.' That's why there is so much tapping up of players by agents, because they're rarely 100 per cent happy.

Signing with a super agent

An agent can only formally sign them at 16 but the reality is the player will very rarely stay with one agent for their whole careers. What usually happens now is a young player will sign with a smaller agent as they progress. Then when they hit the first team or are tipped as a big prospect, suddenly they are blinded by pound signs in front of their very eyes. The next thing everyone knows is that the player has dumped his old agent and signed with a new super agent.

Once they've switched once then the likelihood is that they will be tempted to change again and again throughout their careers. The money to be made is just too tempting and agents end up paying out thousands to get players on board knowing that their investment in the short term will pay off in the long term as players receive big contracts and percentages from transfer fees.

WHAT THE AGENT SAID

Crap deals and compromises

There are so many examples of players and agents having rows and splits. One summer, a Premier League club were all over two players. One was seen as first choice, the other was back-up. The move for the back-up player fell through. It's a hard conversation on deadline day when the agent has to ring up and say: 'Sorry, you're not moving. But don't worry, people are talking about you, you can get a new deal and a better contract.'

A month later, the player rang the agent and said it was time for a change and he would not require the agent's services any longer. The agent asked the player to get his new agent to ring him. 'I haven't got a new agent,' said the player. Yeah, yeah, whatever. Of course he had.

Most agents will not care as long as they get their five per cent. That has to be the attitude. And then, surprise, surprise, six weeks later, the new agent comes on offering a pay-off to the original agent – a compromise and a crap deal.

The first agent was not bothered because he knew if he didn't get the five per cent of any transfer while the player was still under contract then he could just sue. If the new agent really thought he could get away with an 80-20 split of a contract or deal then he had another thing coming.

Then just before the January transfer window opened, a manager rang the original agent and said he wanted to sign the player. The agent had to tell the manager what was going on, there had been a parting of the ways and yet all the manager was interested in was signing the player.

So the original agent went to see the player. He told him he was not taking an 80-20 split, he just wanted his five per cent of what the new club were offering. They hadn't fallen out. It was just business.

The signing club were offering £1m and £14,000-a-week. The player was on less than a third of that at his current club, he'd get a signing-on fee and it was a great deal.

He said he'd think about it. A few hours later the player rang the manager and he said he didn't want to move. The manager was fuming. He then rang the player, the player told him it didn't feel right and he wanted to wait for a better chance in the Premier League.

A year later, the player had switched agents completely, then joined a Championship club with a view to a permanent deal. He was being offered £8,000-a-week.

The player was last seen back on loan at his first club because he couldn't get into his new club's first team. He's had some terrible advice, advice all about making the agent some money. They're not interested in the player and getting the player a good contract.

The new agent would rather tell the player to stay put, lose out financially and miss out on a big deal all because the agent knew he wouldn't get a pay day himself.

That's a classic example of bad advice and tapping up because the new agent has come in and ended up costing the player about £6,000-a-week.

And the craziest thing of all, he's now left the other agent and signed for someone else anyway!

That's happened hundreds of times. It's a sliding doors moment. And you can bet most players get a phone call every week from an agent trying to sign them.

Brutal and ruthless

For many agents, they will be close to a player. They will take the player out for dinner, talk every day, text all the time. Then suddenly, just like that, it stops and the player will not respond to the agent. The ruthless players will not think about it for a second, will not give any hint there's a problem or that someone else is on the scene and making approaches. The first thing the agent will know about it is when suddenly the calls stop, the texts dry up and their player will not even answer the phone when the agent's name pops up. It is brutal and ruthless.

That annoys some agents more than others. It certainly annoys them all at first. But then they become used to it because it is part of football. And they will be comforted by the thought that they have the player under contract.

The player's standard contract with an agent is for two years. Many players will get fed up and try to change their deal during the two years, but no agent worth his salt will step aside while there is still a chance of money to be made.

Approaches from new agents normally happen after it has come to light that there is a problem between the existing agent and his client. The new agent moves in for the kill. Even if one agent is friendly with another it will not matter a jot.

Bluff and hot air

Footballers are impressionable and if they are getting phone calls left, right and centre promising all kinds of riches

they will be tempted and often they will go ahead and sign with predatory agents. Even if there is no deal on the table, the agent will promise the earth to get his man.

I know of one player who was getting three or four calls a day from an agent saying he'd got him a deal, and that if he signed with him then he would get signed up with a club within 48 hours.

The player got completely fed up with being pestered and one day turned round to the agent and said: 'Go on then, prove it.' He never heard from the agent again. It was all utter nonsense. There was no deal. It was complete bluff. All hot air.

In the list of 10 things an agent needs to have, an elephant skin and balls the size of an elephant's are vital. So sure enough the agent tried again and in October rang the player imploring him to sign with him. That's what agents have to be like. They have got to be very determined in this game. But the incredible thing is that the agent eventually persuaded the player to sign. He'd promised him a non-existent deal, let him down and then disappeared. A few months later he came back, still pursued him and still signed him up as a client.

All in the family

Some players do begrudge agents their cut and it's why an increasing number are choosing to be represented by family members.

This is a relatively new thing and a large part of it is because the player would rather the agent's slice of the pie from a transfer fee or contract goes to their brother, dad or whoever. Just as long as it's not an agent who they think is either going to rip them off or not do a very good job.

Relatives are also getting more and more involved because the potential financial rewards in football are so ridiculous and the openness of the market to become an agent. Dads become greedy, thinking the work of an agent is easy and they can do it. But when realise it's not so easy, and they don't know it all, it can be a nasty shock.

Not many people outside of the industry know about the tax and benefit in kind and the P11D. If someone works on behalf of a footballer, and he is signed and registered with the FA, the player has to pay 40 per cent tax on the agent fee as a P11D benefit in kind.

Dads who want to be involved have no idea that if they get a £100,000 agent fee from moving their son from one club to another then their son has to pay £40,000 in tax.

That change was made about three or four years ago. There was never a tax implication on the player, until HMRC decided an agent fee was a benefit in kind. The club still pays the agent fee on the player's behalf and he pays it to the agent. But the player still ends up with the tax bill because it's seen as a benefit in kind.

HMRC decided to then start charging players and because most players earn over £50,000-a-year then it is levied at 40 per cent.

What generally happens is that, for example, if the agent fee is £100,000 then it is paid out over the course of the contract, £25,000 per year and then the player will get a tax bill of 40 per cent of about £10,000-a-year. That's down to the player to pay;

they have to pay that every year.

The tax implication for the player is big and then their dad or the new intermederies – as they are now called – don't know. They don't know the rules, they don't know these implications.

The player thinks their dad knows them best, looks out for them, has got their best interests at heart – and then they're landed with a £40,000 tax bill because the dad doesn't know the first thing about being an agent!

They are the sort of pitfalls that you don't know about unless you are a professional and know your job.

Taxing times

Football can be a murky world with gangsters, greedy agents and backhanders. But sometimes being looked after by your own dad can be even

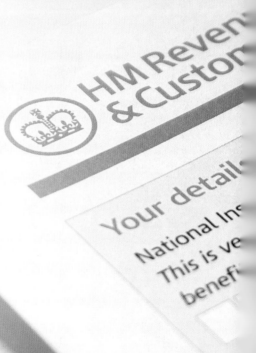

worse if he doesn't know the first thing about the business. A player's future can be shaped by one bad deal, or a deal hinging on whether the agent stands to make a few quid rather than because it's better for the player himself.

Of course, some agents are seen as fly-by-nights or just flash without knowing anything or having real expertise. But they are still the professionals – they have the contacts and the know-how to get deals done.

Many of the parents now acting as agents get their knowledge from watching their sons play on a Sunday morning.

That's their extent of knowledge of the business.

There are some bad agents as well, and too many greedy ones, looking for their cut. Some high-profile players of the past have discovered they are not quite as rich as they had been told they were going to be. Now, the taxman is clamping down on footballers. He has targeted the industry and is determined to get his cut as well.

Players are being hit from all sides. If it's not the agent then it's the taxman.

Having someone who can operate finances with your best interests at heart, will stand you in good stead. (Shutterstock)

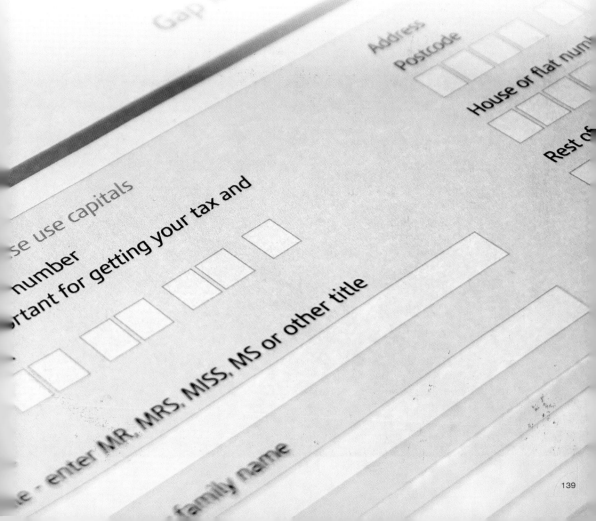

11

FOREIGN FIELDS

Just think of how many foreign players there are in the Premier League. In fact, no-one can forget because either the Football Association, England managers or the media are always reminding us. But when it comes to big, money spinning, glamorous deals abroad, there seems to be an incredible reluctance among British players to try their luck in Italy, Spain or Germany. There are fantastic opportunities to play abroad for British players but all too few take up the chance.

Culture clash

There have been very, very few players who – at the peak of their powers rather than those looking for a last pay day – have tried their luck abroad.

Back in the 1980s and 1990s, players of the calibre of Liam Brady, Graeme Souness, Ian Rush and Ray Wilkins went overseas. Some liked it. Or some, as in Ian Rush's case, couldn't get home soon enough.

David Beckham went, or more to the point, was pushed out of the door by Sir Alex Ferguson when Manchester United sold him to Real Madrid.

So, why don't more players go abroad? Language and lifestyle are factors that deter such switches, and it is almost seen as unusual for a top British player to go abroad. Big players do not even go to America in their prime so it is even less likely that they would want to go somewhere in Europe where they can't speak the language.

A generation ago, circumstances were different. It used to be that a player would start at a club in England, move to a bigger club, become a huge success and then consider going abroad. In the 1980s wages were better in Italy and life was more glamorous in Spain. But with

the Premier League now the richest in the world and able, as a whole, to pay the largest salaries, there is not the same incentive to seek pastures new.

Foreign invasion

The 1990s witnessed a foreign invasion because the money in the Premier League suddenly provided a lure to foreign players

The flying boot incident with Sir Alex Ferguson, that left David Beckham with a cut over his eye, may have contributed to his move to Real Madrid in 2003. (Shutterstock)

to come here. Big-name players of the calibre of Gianfranco Zola and Dennis Bergkamp came to England.

In the last 10 years or so, the bigger Spanish clubs have shown they can still compete financially. PSG in France and Bayern Munich in Germany have taken a number of the major players who used to move to the Premier League to La Liga, Ligue 1 and the Bundesliga.

But the British players have also decided to stay put rather than go abroad even though the top clubs in Spain and a few others elsewhere can pay big money just like the Premier League. What used to be a dream and an adventure of moving abroad for the likes of Gary Lineker and Mark Hughes, has now become a rarity.

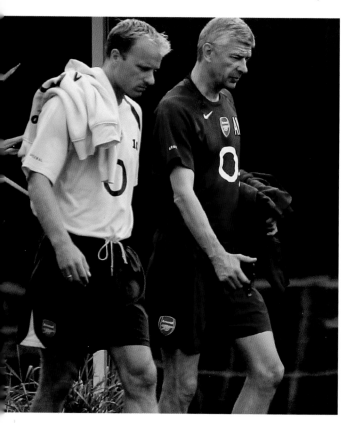

British attitudes

The biggest obstacle is the change of lifestyle. Most players will not want to move their lives, their family and their world abroad. That is a very parochial, very British attitude. Some players will struggle to learn the language. Understandably, coaches want players to be able to communicate effectively. But while English is a second tongue for many foreign players, their British counterparts have difficulty in picking up the same language skills. Differences in culture and customs also work against British players playing and living abroad.

Random and bizarre

But such moves by British players do still occur. Gareth Bale was in a sense bought against his club's wishes. Tottenham

did not want to sell him. But once sums approaching £90m were mentioned, they soon changed their mind. The club did not drive the deal, whereas in the case of Beckham United wanted to sell.

Michael Owen's move to Real was a little bizarre. Similarly, Jonathan Woodgate's move to Madrid was totally random. It is very rare, because clubs here are so rich that the best players will not be tempted abroad. They end up at Arsenal, Chelsea, Manchester City or Manchester United, who can pay broadly the same as Real Madrid.

Broadening horizons

For a British player who had played for his country and earned a very good living,

then chances are that he will not want to leave the Premier League. This has been the situation in the last 20 years or so with more players wanting to stay put. There are accusations levelled at them that they are insular and unwilling to broaden their horizons. That attitude can hold a player back from being even more successful.

Now it would seem as if there is a small change in the air with a few moving to the MLS, offers from China and also from Italy and Spain. But it's still a slow process.

Limited ambitions

Looking at the next potential superstars illustrates the point. Ross Barkley came through at Everton, burst onto the scene, played for England, and became a much sought-after talent. The same applied to

Gary Lineker (right) and Mark Hughes made all the headlines when they transferred to Barcelona in 1986. (Getty)

143

Gareth Bale with
his man bun
has made an
impact playing
for Real Madrid.
(Shutterstock)

John Stones, who came from Barnsley, went to Everton and was then sold for huge money to Manchester City. It is unlikely either would have been saying to their agents that they want to go abroad and play for Real Madrid or Barcelona. That is not to say they would not do so, but more a case of what their practical aims are. Stones wanted to go to Chelsea in the summer of 2015, but ended up at Manchester City a year later. It showed he was and is ambitious but wants to stay in the Premier League. There's a limit to those ambitions.

Others will make a foreign move work for them. Liam Ridgewell was not in the top-talent bracket but he went to the MLS, captained his team to cup-winning success, and the move worked out brilliantly for him. Ridgewell is not top class, by any means, but has had a brilliant end to his career. Bradley Wright-Phillips could not get a game for Charlton in the Championship. He secured a very good move to New York Red Bulls, became a DP (designated player under the MLS rules) and would earn about ten times what he earned at Charlton.

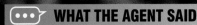

WHAT THE AGENT SAID

Booze bender

There is an accepted wisdom that foreign players are more professional and focused. Running alongside that is the glib acceptance of the old adage that English players like a drink. In truth these days not many English players go out on big benders and get smashed. So they have the odd drink now and again. Well, is that really that different for foreign players? You can't tell me that a foreign player won't have the odd glass of wine or even the odd French player has a cigarette. It's not that unusual.

There's talk that one top striker in the Premier League loves a night out and drinks a lot. But he's a foreigner. There's another top player who has suddenly put on a bit of weight. He's foreign, a top star and yet suddenly he can't get round the pitch like he did. Is he more focused or professional than an English player?

Does going out, having a bite to eat, a glass of wine with your meal, make you less professional or focused? No. A lot is said about foreign players being more focused but that is not necessarily true.

There's a culture in English football where the boys go out together, have meals together, big nights out and it makes for good unity and shows camaraderie. Does that happen abroad? Yes. But not as much as it happens here. When Alexis Sanchez first came to Arsenal, it must have taken him some time before he made friends, became one of the boys and started going out with other players for a bite to eat. It's a different culture.

When Gareth Bale was signed by Real Madrid, it was full of 'Galacticos' – the truly world-class superstars, so it would have taken him a few months to realise who he got on with – whether, for example, he could become friends with Cristiano Ronaldo. But Bale is still an exception in terms of British players going abroad. He was at the peak of his powers at a big club in Tottenham, but when a superclub like Real Madrid come knocking, it is the pinnacle and players do not turn them down.

There are agents in England driving deals to the MLS and a Chinese agent working here in England trying to get players to China. The big agencies like Stellar, WMG and Base are all looking to get a foothold in the Chinese market. Chinese clubs are focused on buying attackers and not defenders. They want the glamour signings. But as the market expands, that will change and the number of players and agents wanting a piece of the action will grow and grow.

China calling

These are the foreign leagues that are tempting British players. The MLS in America is very attractive and is firmly on the radar for a lot of players, but it is still more for those who are coming to the end of their careers and looking for a last – and very well-paid – adventure.

Playing for the New York Red Bulls, Bradley Wright-Phillips. (Shutterstock)

Steven Gerrard's move to the MLS was player driven. He had given fantastic service for 15 years over here, and after a great career went for one last pay day.

China is coming into play now, and no big British players have gone there yet at the peak of their powers. But there are agents in the UK trying to work on the Chinese market where the perception is that money is no obstacle. The Chinese government has signalled that the

spending by Chinese clubs will be reined in, but the potential financial rewards are still huge.

Money is, of course, always a big draw. But if a young player like Alex Oxlade-Chamberlain was offered £100,000-a-week to stay at Arsenal compared to £200,000-a-week in China, he would probably stay in England. At the moment, the Chinese league is in its infancy, the playing standard is not particularly good and it is difficult for Chinese clubs to make signings of a certain type of player.

Other factors complicate the picture. Some younger players, like the Colombian Jackson Martinez and Brazilian Alex Teixeira, have gone to China. A lot of the players are represented by very big and influential agents. Third party ownership was banned by the English FA in 2008 largely after the Javier Mascherano and Carlos Tevez deals. A global ban on third party ownership of players was introduced by FIFA in 2015. But agents have found loopholes including buying shares in a club, with a view to cashing in with a cut of transfer fees netted by the club; and being repaid plus 'interest' from sell-on fees; and then acting as an agent to get a bigger commission. There is so much money at stake for the agents that they will put huge pressure on players to go and sign lucrative deals.

There are many strange deals in football. Look at Chelsea's deal for Alexandre Pato in 2016. He was a big name but Chelsea said he wasn't fit enough to play. So, why sign him? He only played twice and then left.

Blocked passage

One consequence of so many foreign players coming to England is that it reduces opportunities for young British players to come through. What chance has a 19-year-old at Chelsea if they are signing Pato? But as with any signing, someone loses out. Often it will be the younger domestic players because big or ageing signings will block their path.

We're all talking about young British players coming through. They all want a chance, though not always for the best reasons. There's a kid in the Championship, who was called up into the first team squad. He got on the bench but didn't get on the pitch during the game. His first reaction? He said, 'I'm gutted, I won't get my bonus.'

But, as a nation, we've got to give our young players a chance. It's a shame when foreign players, probably washed up and past it, come over here and block the passage of our young players. So it shouldn't just be about players leaving the Premier League to go abroad for one last pay day or retirement plan. We wouldn't like it the other way round, so it would be nice to see our players go abroad at the peak of their powers, when they are at their best to push themselves, be ambitious and go to play at the highest level in the Champions League.

Bale bailed out

Many of today's English stars could be the next to go. But will they go abroad? The law of averages suggests not. Bale is the exception to the rule. It is incredible to think of all the players, of all the talent, only one has gone to a superclub. Bale wanted to go to Real Madrid, the biggest club in the world. There is no certainty however, that any home-grown talented player will make the move abroad.

La Liga Land

Real Madrid and Barcelona can compete financially with the Premier League and are virtually guaranteed success. The big two also get 80 per cent of the TV money in Spain.

There was a trend for players to come to England as Premier League clubs paid more but now that has levelled out. There are huge riches at the big clubs in Spain and the Premier League misses out on global superstars. Cristiano Ronaldo went to Real Madrid and Luis Suarez left Liverpool for Barcelona.

After having paid his dues at Liverpool, Steven Gerrard headed for the USA before embarking on management.
(Shutterstock)

Luis Suarez visiting his old stamping ground, Liverpool's Melwood training ground. (Getty)

Teddy Sheringham (second from right) and Andy Cole (far right) clashed personality wise. (Getty)

Can they cut it?

There is an argument to be made that the British game in any case does not suit many foreign players, particularly from southern Europe. There is definite resentment among English players about some of the foreign imports. They get a bit jealous and annoyed when they hear all the talk about how great the foreigners are, how they train professionally, don't drink and so on.

WHAT THE AGENT SAID

Premier League own goal

The Premier League is an undeniably gruelling competition. It is worth considering whether Iniesta or Toni Kroos would be as good at international tournaments for their countries if they played their club football in the Premier League. They do not have it as physically demanding as the players in the Premier League, in terms of games, intensity and the lack of a winter break.

That means British players are a little bit more tired when they come to the end of the season. Foreign internationals play in England of course, but not all of them. In Spain, they might have two or three who play in the Premier League and they can be carried. In Germany, it's Ozil and again the German national side can accommodate him even if he has had a hard, long season.

But on the pitch, the English lads often say the foreign players do not want to know about hard 50-50 tackles, or when the going gets tough. The English lads think they have a better spirit and they fight for each other on the pitch. They think the foreign boys don't, as the saying goes 'always put it on the pitch'. Of course there are exceptions to the rule like Diego Costa or Luis Suarez. But generally, there is a perception that adheres to stereotypes: the English lads are all about the bulldog spirit, the foreign lads are fancy Dans.

Scott Dann and Damien Delaney proved to be good, solid pros at Crystal Palace without being flash. Their game has much to do with guts and determination. Are they any worse than an expensive foreign player? Would a foreign player who cost a lot of money do better at Palace?

A wet Wednesday in Stoke

If Lionel Messi came into the English game would he be as good week-in and week-out as he is in Spain? Could he, as the cliché goes, manage to cut it on a wet Wednesday in Stoke? Was Cristiano Ronaldo as good and as prolific when he was at Manchester

United as he has been in Spain? Was Luis Suarez as effective for Liverpool as he has when signing for Barcelona?

These are the accusatory questions levelled at foreign talent. Of course, the reason why Suarez flourished at Barcelona is that the team are very good at providing plenty of chances for their forwards. And Messi's and Ronaldo's talent is undeniable.

But the English game is much more physical. The Championship in England is stronger than in any other second division across the world. No other league is like that. It also compares unbelievably well in terms of finance.

Why leave the best league in the world?

In terms of a British player going abroad, there are factors that work against it happening. But the biggest single reason as to why more British players don't go abroad is down to money. The Premier League is the best league in the world, it pays the most and the players stay here because they can earn more.

Elitist

It will always be the case that a handful of British players pop up at obscure clubs, in different leagues. It would be nice to see a top Championship player go to an average French team, as it would encourage Premier League clubs to be less elitist and be more open to signing players from the lower divisions. If a player, for example, went to Lorient and was successful then more clubs in England would sit up and take notice.

Steven Fletcher went to Marseille, as did Joey Barton. It helped them develop and is a good illustration of why the domestic game as a whole needs to broaden its horizons.

Dressing room feuds

Of course not every player likes one another. But it's rarely anything to do with nationality – just petty dressing room feuds or a clash of personalities. Some probably want to escape a teammate they do not like or they want to try something new. In fact, it's been well documented down the years that there's been teams with players who don't get on. Just look at Andy Cole and Teddy Sheringham. They didn't like each other, didn't speak to each other but they won the Treble together. That tells you that you can be professional. Do your job, be focused and professional on the pitch and within that group of Man United players, there would have been cliques. When Andy Cole went out, he had his mates and Teddy Sheringham had his mates. They were all probably mates with each other but knew that Teddy and Andy didn't get on. If they all went out for a night, they'd go out with whoever they got on with. It's always been the same.

Footballers don't really socialise outside their little network of friends. The culture of football is supposed to be the game of the people. But footballers don't mix with the people, they all socialise with each other. It's the same the world over. They all have the same mates in England, they share the same friends, go to the same nightclubs and restaurants.

BIG BUSINESS

People seemed really shocked when Kenny Sansom was pictured down-and-out, sleeping rough on a park bench with only a bottle of booze to keep him company. We have this image of footballers being made for life, multi-millionaires and incredibly wealthy thanks to their earnings from the beautiful game.

But here's the thing. When Sansom was playing for Arsenal and England, the players were paid a fraction of what they earn now. Sansom had a great career, had big moves, played for Arsenal, Crystal Palace, Queens Park Rangers and Newcastle among others, plus he won 86 caps for England.

He was the best left back of his generation. But he was at the top of the game before the multi-million-pound Premier League contracts kicked in. He was not made for life. It's a million miles away from the big players of today and when he hit the bottle people seemed more surprised that a top footballer was living on the streets than because he had become an alcoholic.

Investing for the future

An idea persists that footballers are hard-drinking party animals. The majority are not. Many are teetotal, live respectably and are sensible with their money.

Kenny Sansom (far left) in happier times with the England 1982 squad. Left to right: Sansom, Steve Foster, Trevor Francis, Steve Coppell, Ray Clemence, Graham Rix, Joe Corrigan and Glenn Hoddle. (Getty)

Many players think about a career that means they stay in the game and take their coaching badges. Others set up successful businesses, in order to prepare themselves for retirement. Some take a few risks here and there with investments because they have so much money they can afford to throw the odd million or two at a more adventurous business deal. From buying up houses to rent out to spending big money on stocks and shares, footballers have so much money they don't know quite what to do with it.

A number of players have set up fashion brands – Cristiano Ronaldo has done so with his CR7 label. He promoted it on the *Jonathan Ross Show*. Others have bought into foreign property, websites and restaurants, bars and nightclubs. It doesn't matter if these ventures are not all profitable. The attitude is 'there's a few million more where that came from'.

In some players that attitude can get out of hand and they become reckless with their spending on cars, houses and holidays. Outsiders might see it as having more money than sense. But, in reality, players generally come from humble beginnings. They were not born with too

💬 WHAT THE AGENT SAID

The life of Riley

Here's a little illustration about how football earnings can be transformative and not just at the elite level. A run-of-the-mill Championship striker was on £10,000-a-week and a £10,000-per-goal bonus. He scored a hat-trick in one game and took home £40,000 that week. Nice work if you can get it.

As soon as the Premier League era kicked in, players were set up for life with one big contract. Now they can be set up for life with one deal in the Championship. A three-year contract guarantees enormous income. Even the smallest Premier League contracts pay £20,000-a-week. That means £3m guaranteed.

The hope is that the recipient will be able to live comfortably for the rest of their days. If the money is invested wisely, for example in property and prices rise as they have done for decades, then a player will be worth a lot more than that £3m and he should be living the life of Riley. And that's not taking into account things like signing-on fees, appearance money, loyalty bonuses and image rights. Football is life-changing. It can make anyone, any family, rich and that's why players are so determined to earn as much as they can.

many advantages in life other than they had an innate talent for football, and yet they've earned millions. It is unfair to expect them to be too careful and shrewd with money. But we can expect them to enjoy their new-found wealth and most certainly do.

Care of duty

It is possible to have some sympathy with footballers because if agents are themselves earning huge sums from their clients and the clubs then they have to show some duty of care. If a player blows it all, is it all down to the player? Or do the people and the business around him have some responsibility? Perhaps the Professional Footballers' Association should have more input. But the agent can only do so much. There has to be a realisation from the players that they have to think about looking after themselves. Of course, they are told about pensions, but what can any agent do if his client does not want to listen?

There has got to be a little bit of responsibility. 'You're a grown man now, mate,' the agent should be telling the player. For someone who has played at the highest level then it will not matter if he doesn't work for another 50 years because he'll have enough money to comfortably live on for the rest of his life.

Teenage riches

There are deals happening now with the big clubs for average teenagers with Premier League potential. They are being offered first-year pro contracts for £125,000-a-year, guaranteed. Imagine being 14 and told a wage of £125,000 is within your grasp. It's incredible. It might not be the stuff of millionaires

just yet, but at 14, knowing you'll soon be earning £125,000-a-year while your mates will be unemployed or earning peanuts on zero-hour contracts, you can be forgiven for getting a little bit carried away.

Poor little rich kids

At the big clubs the wages spent on youngsters can almost be categorised as compensation. Many of these kids are not going to play in the Premier League. Some of the young pros are on £20,000-a-week by the time they hit 18 and yet are nowhere near the first team. It is something of a scattergun approach from the clubs. They want the best kids, and so pay them the best money and if one suddenly progresses and steps up then the gamble has paid off.

Some talented teenagers are now being dangled a money carrot by the football clubs.
(Shutterstock)

💬 WHAT THE AGENT SAID

Hidden dangers

There can be a problem in making the adjustment to a non-playing – and therefore non-earning – life, however. People want to live a lifestyle that they become accustomed to. They love luxury, amazing cars, nice houses and incredible holidays. That's not exclusive to football – any Tom, Dick or Harry in the street would go out and spend like there was no tomorrow if they were given that kind of money.

There is always a danger of overspending for footballers, again because of their ludicrous tendency to engage in one-upmanship. They spend money just to show off. They will always push themselves and spend sometimes beyond even their means, very quickly.

💬 WHAT THE AGENT SAID

First £100m transfer between Premier League clubs

£100m transfers in the Premier League are just around the corner. That's because every club in the world knows the Premier League has just secured an £8billion TV deal. It follows the basic principles of supply and demand.

For years, the talk has been of the 'football bubble' bursting. Commentators keep saying wages cannot keep rising as much as they are as fast as they are. And yet they keep going up and up. The money keeps rolling in with ever-increasing TV rights. Increasing competition between the broadcasters is pushing the price up even further.

It is the same across the whole of football. An agent needs one big deal. A player needs one big contract. A club can get £50m for a player not worth anywhere near that.

The hangers-on are incredible and that's because of the money. And they'll do anything that needs fixing. For example, there are players who get drink driving bans. He goes to one of his mates, if he's earning £500-a-week being a builder, the player can pay him £600-a-week to drive him everywhere. They will get them to come and live with them, look after them and most footballers will have a mate running around for them. They will literally have a runner because the money is astronomical. Even at £20,000-a-week, you can afford to give someone £500-a-week to drive them around or run errands. A top player will have go-fers and hangers-on doing everything from errands, shopping to getting them on the best VIP list at nightclubs.

Players get investment offers, all sorts of scams and businesses pushed their way all the time. So much of the time one player follows another like a sheep.

One big player took his agent into the England team hotel. He'd done well in property deals, told them they could buy into it and they'd get even richer. Sadly, some of these went badly wrong and the money went down the drain.

Living life for free

The irony is that when people become very wealthy, suddenly so many things become free. Players get top-of-the-range supercars, vehicles worth upwards of £100,000 for free just so they can drive it around and be seen driving them. Premier League players will go into coffee shops, pubs or wherever and suddenly the barman or the staff behind the counter are saying: 'This one's on the house.'

There are freebies, holidays, trips and cars left, right and centre. Stick your name on this, endorse this, and they get treated like kings. They don't have to put their hand in an already bulging pocket. The wealth now is a different level to the days of Kenny Sansom and the rest. Of course falls from grace can happen to the elite players of today. But their earnings are on a different scale and should be enough to compensate for any problems later in life.

Tricks

Players get hoodwinked by hangers-on trying to trick them into investing in some hare-brained scheme. Players have to be careful and that's why it's so dangerous to have dads or relatives involved as agents. They become too emotionally involved.

Down the river

The loyalty between players and agents can change as players get older and begin

WHAT THE AGENT SAID

A piece of the action

A night out with footballers is an experience. They are roped off into VIP areas in bars and clubs and the place is overloaded with hangers-on. They are there to be seen with a footballer, ply them with free drinks and do anything to get in with the in-crowd. It can be embarrassing to watch these people acting as if they are the player's best mate. Everyone wants to jump on the bandwagon, they all want a piece of the football action.

to wind down their careers – and thus their earning potential. It can cause major problems for both player and agent.

The climate of mistrust, whereby a player has shown little or no loyalty down the years, means it works against the possibility of an agent going out of his way to do what is best for the player.

If there's a last bit of extra cash to be earned, an agent will earn it the best way he can and will not hesitate to sell a player down the river. The game is full of stories of players complaining their agent didn't do well for them in the latter part of their career.

Money from all angles

The backhanders and inducements from agents have now become so big – cars and huge amounts of money – that it is yet another way of getting rich quick for the already highly paid footballer. Money is coming at them from all angles.

They are incredible sums of money and that's why you can see why footballers on big Premier League contracts never really have to worry about the future. If they are sensible, then they are made for life. But, let's be honest, the temptation is to roll the dice and become even wealthier.

Moving on

The huge stakes on offer can make the player and the agent greedy. It can make them ready to move a bit more often, chase another contract, another big money move, another commission or signing-on fee.

The millions soon stack up and yet the greed is the biggest reason why you get such little loyalty whether it's one player staying at a club for life, staying with one agent or asking for a transfer. Everyone is chasing the next quick buck.

If you leave and change jobs every year then will you ever have a relationship with your boss? No. It's the same in football.

Does a recruitment consultant have a relationship with their clients? No. Because they all move on. That's the hard truth.

'Weighed in'

Now, for many agents, they see the player as a commodity. It's like they have a player for the summer, the agent tries to move them on, earn a commission, get a deal and then the player leaves the agent anyway.

Some agents want to get 'weighed in'. They are more interested in getting a fast buck because the player will move on anyway. The unscrupulous agents don't worry about the player in the longer term. Does the agent then really care whether they are still earning at 35? No, of course not. It's a short career.

••• ◗ WHAT THE AGENT SAID

Chop and change

Some players stay with their agents for life. Look at Ryan Giggs, he stayed with Harry Swales for years and years. The thing is, who is Harry Swales? He's a nobody in agent terms. Sir Alex Ferguson introduced and recommended him as a good agent, someone who was down to earth, sensible and would be a good guide for his career. It proved a pretty good relationship.

But loyalty Is becoming less and less common. Loyalty is rare in an age before it became pounds, shillings and pence.

There are new obstacles to earnings and retirement plans. One of the biggest pitfalls is the taxman because, while no agent would admit that he assists his clients in trying to avoid tax, they are fully aware that the taxman has looked at football and even he wants a piece of the action. This has caught some players unawares and given them a rude shock.

As we have seen, benefits in kind are one such trap that has tripped up players and agents. It creates an opportunity for agents to use such problems against each other. An agent will tell a player that he would have ensured the player was not going to be caught out by the taxman. 'Oh, we would have paid that for you,' one agent might say to a player to try and persuade him to leave his current agent.

So many times recently there have been stories where players feel they've been done on tax. They haven't really, but they feel as if they have. And the first person to blame is their agent.

There is a suggestion one famous player left his agent because he got a whacking great tax bill. It was no-one's fault, certainly not the agent, because everyone has to pay tax, but even very wealthy footballers don't like giving money away. The player and his representatives had a row over a tax bill which they think should have been paid by the agent.

This is all a relatively new thing. There have been stories of a few agents gunning for players because their complaints about tax and the blame being put on agents have come out in the dressing room. Other agents will get wind of it, ring the aggrieved player and offer to pay the tax bill. But that tells you very little about whether they are good agents or not – it just tells you that they'll pay your tax bill.

13

THE END GAME

It is tough out there beyond the football bubble. When players finish their playing careers, they suddenly wake up and realise they have to survive in the real world. Except today, the goalposts have been moved because many players do not have to find another job. They are so wealthy, and have made so much money that they never have to work again. Some will, however, work again. If they've squandered their earnings, if they didn't quite hit the big time or they simply need the buzz. Football is an addiction that some just can't shake off.

Welcome to management

Gone are the days when players immediately looked to become managers (or failing that, become a taxi driver telling passengers about the good old days). But the fun really does stop when the playing days are over if you are crazy – or desperate – enough to go into management.

'You're useless!'

One manager, in his first job, was really struggling at a club and was under all sorts of pressure from a mad owner and chairman. They lost a game, the chairman came in, the manager left him to it and the chairman went bonkers at the players, tore them off a strip, went crazy and then the manager walked back in. The chairman then turns on the manager and says: 'You're f***ing useless as well!'. Welcome to management.

That manager should have told the chairman to stick it there and then to keep any sort of authority. But he couldn't because it might have damaged his chances of getting another job, as it was his one shot at making it in the managerial

game. Yet it was a sure sign he was not going to last and within a few weeks he was out of a job anyway. The dressing room dressing down was in front of all the staff, the coaches, the players – everyone. It meant he was a dead man walking.

Media matters

The nature of football management has always been crazy, and managers have always been on a hiding to nothing. But in recent years it has become an impossible job with no job security. That's why the new generation who have earned big money are going into the media.

Gary Neville went into TV before eventually taking the coaching route. Jamie Carragher has surely got so much to offer but went into TV after retiring. From the recent England generation, very few want to go into coaching. Scott Parker is one of the very few to buck the trend. Parker has taken his coaching badges and was rewarded with a youth coaching role at his old club Spurs.

TV times

But more often players look to get into the media with Sky, BT Sport, talkSPORT, the

Football management for former players isn't for everyone. Many, however, excel in the 'pressure cooker' environment. (Shutterstock)

BBC. They see Gary Neville, Carragher, Thierry Henry and Robbie Savage having a great life and want to follow suit as TV stars.

There seems to be room for everyone because there are so many radio and TV shows now talking about football 24/7. It's an easier way to stay involved with the game which is something they must want because if they've been sensible, their money has, or at least should, be ring-fenced and they should never be short of money.

Tough adjustment

An alternative to management is to become an agent, or work with agents to scout or recruit players.

Former players now spend their time talent-spotting players; they do it to try and stay in the business. It means they can go and scout games, run into people in directors' boxes and stadiums all while watching football. It provides that connection with the game they would lose in retirement.

A lot of players find it very hard after retirement. Tony Cascarino, the former Republic of Ireland striker, said a lot of players get divorced afterwards but the reality is that wives and partners get accustomed to the lifestyle and the players can get fed up, bored and difficult to live with after they hang up their boots because nothing can fill the void and the buzz from playing.

Why bother?

Sadly, more and more players are going out of the game rather than staying in football to become managers. Once upon a time, it was the obvious career path. Now, why would a multi-millionaire actually want the hassle and stress of being a manager? They don't need it.

Even run-of-the-mill players, who at best earned £20,000-a-week, can live in Spain with their families quite comfortably. They can just live off his earnings and afford not to work anymore. They simply don't need the hassle. Management has become treacherous and players do not see it as the next logical step.

Hassle

Players buy their big house, get another house paid for and suddenly they've got £5m worth of property. They are generally very rich if they've invested and spent wisely. In that situation there is little logic in going into a high-risk, high-stress job like football management.

Falling out of love

Every fan thinks every player must love the game. But the uncomfortable truth is different. Some players don't even like football. It may have earned them millions, but they have long since fallen out of love with the game – if they ever loved it in the first place.

And when they retire, some will never go to another game in their lives because they want to make a clean break. Going to football is the last thing they want to do.

They move into investments, stockbroking or similar projects because they've got money to throw around.

Retirement is boring

Some players cannot stand even the thought of retiring and then doing nothing. After a while, rattling around their mansion, taking holidays in Dubai or driving the latest Ferrari lose their appeal. It becomes boring. What will players do with all their time? And coming from a busy, high-energy way of life where they are training every day, playing sport and being ultra-competitive, it's difficult to switch off to nothing.

📢 WHAT THE AGENT SAID

Stop hanging around

Jamie Carragher clearly has great enthusiasm for the game, extensive knowledge, and has been a very good pundit, but has clearly avoided coaching.

Gary Neville is a bit different having tried coaching and doing his fair share of TV. He has shown a drive and a determination to be a manager. It has not worked out for him so far after his ill-starred spell as manager of Valencia in Spain, but the hunger appears to still be there in him.

Something slightly different happened with Thierry Henry. His old Arsenal manager Arsène Wenger did not want him to be a coach at the Emirates and a TV pundit so gave him an ultimatum. Henry decided to stay with Sky rather than become a coach with his beloved Arsenal. His £5m-a-year contract at Sky compared to maybe £150,000-a-year at Arsenal as a youth coach might have had something to do with it. Henry has since gone on to reignite his coaching desires for the Belgium national team.

But it is a great shame that some of the biggest names, with the most enthusiasm, are slipping out of the game. Sadly, they don't need the hassle anymore. They are too wealthy, too comfortable, and management or coaching is just too tough.

It probably hits boxers harder than footballers because that sport is so intense, with the training and the intensity of fights. But equally it is hard to be in the limelight as a footballer and then retire and do nothing.

Learning the ropes

The vast majority of big-name players probably want to start their managerial careers at a high level. Credit must therefore be given to Teddy Sheringham, a big player who won the Treble with Manchester United and played at the highest level with England. But when he started out as a manager, he went to Stevenage Borough.

WHAT THE AGENT SAID

Home banker

You've got £10m in the bank but you still want to earn to keep topping it up. That's just a natural way of life. Some players have got £10m in the bank, but they don't want to spend the next 30 years spending their money. They want to keep money coming in, topping up the pot. They're happy to take a risk, put their fortune on the line, and get back the buzz they used to have on the pitch.

It is a bug, an addiction. The buzz of being in football is irresistible. A lot of lesser players go into management because they couldn't reach the top, play for Manchester United as a player but they want to go on and manage them instead.

Maybe the top players go into punditry because they've got less to prove and more money to enjoy. Football and being a football manager can be non-stop torture. But it's easier in the media.

But maybe lesser players go into management because they didn't earn fortunes which mean they can't retire. They need to keep going, to pay for their mortgage and family. That means they remain hungry, driven and determined. Lee Johnson is a good example. He's carving out a good career as a manager. He did OK at Oldham, got the Barnsley job, he lost nine out of 10 games, but they stuck by him, to the credit of the owners at Barnsley. He won seven on the trot and then he got the Bristol City job. It's amazing. Good luck to him. That's fantastic and a great advert for what a player can do after their playing days have finished.

Sadly for him that did not work out and he did not last a season.

Tipped

It can be very tough. Gary Neville's first senior job as a manager – or coach on the continent – was at Valencia. Even Neville said himself that he would be questioning the appointment if it was someone else.

Neville had already been Roy Hodgson's No2 with England, had been tipped to be the England manager and here he was at one of Europe's biggest clubs because, the perception at least, was that he was friendly with the Valencia owner, Peter Lim. Again, even Neville – despite being a friend of the owner's – did not last the season.

One shot

A lot of former players will only get one crack at making it as a manager. They will not make it and not get another chance. The League Managers' Association statistics tell us that 70 per cent of

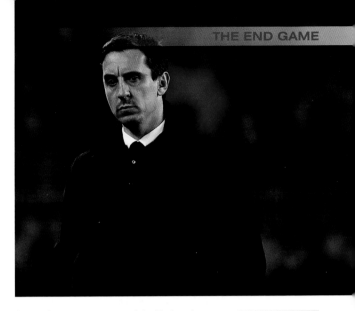

managers who lose their job don't get a second opportunity. Some don't even get a first chance.

Others can't even get an interview because, more than ever, there is so much competition for jobs in management and coaching. And qualifications are important.

A lot of players who leave their playing careers now take the badges and complete the UEFA Pro Licence. Some do it with the Welsh FA rather than in England because it can be cheaper but also easier to get on the course. The Welsh FA almost try to fast-track former players onto their courses as they believe a career in the game means they have got experience and deserve a place.

 WHAT THE AGENT SAID

'Don't you know who I am?'

One former England player sat in a conference with a few football bigwigs – Football Association top brass – for a discussion as to why more top players were not going into management. He had won titles, dozens of England caps, and was one of the best players of his generation. So, the FA wanted to know why he didn't want to move into management.

The player complained that he applied for a job but didn't even get an interview at a Championship club. When it was pointed out that he hadn't completed all his badges, he just came back with a 'don't you know who I am' reply.

Some footballers take the arrogance of their playing careers into management and think they should be given an easy ticket to the top. It should not work like that.

Some former pros complain it's harder to get onto the English FA courses even though the English FA maintain they have the highest possible standards.

The X Box generation

One issue is that tomorrow's managers are coming from a very different generation – the kids that supposedly gave up playing football in the streets because they had the distractions of a PlayStation or an X Box. If they really are that way inclined, will they really be bothered about management? It's hard to believe they will be, especially when earnings from playing are going through the roof.

Determined

The best players reached the top by being driven and determined. But once the playing days finish, they don't need to find jobs in football like previous generations. So it will be more important than ever for those that are persistently the hungriest, and remain so when they finish playing, are the ones to come through into management.

No one said this was going to be easy, especially for Gary Neville at Valencia. (Getty)

Better manager than player? Lee Johnson has shown grit and determination to get the job done for his team. (Getty)

Seen by many as the benchmark for greatness, Lionel Messi. (Shutterstock)

A new era

The odd appearance on Sky or BT wearing a designer suit is one thing. But wearing a tracksuit and looking stressed out on the touchline is quite another.

It is a new era for the elite professional now. They have had a wonderful career, a privileged path into a top club, have earned millions from a young age, had a wonderful lifestyle, and played for club and country if they've reached the top.

Still dreaming

Then a big money foreign move is on offer. And then comes the retirement plan with one last contract as they wind down abroad.

It is a dream life, an incredible living and if they are managed and live right, they are made for life.

It is still *the* best job and no wonder so many kids are still dreaming of becoming a professional footballer. You can start out as a five-year-old, get spotted, go through the academy and the dream of that first team debut.

It is an incredible journey with so many pitfalls and dangers from the fear of being released to the dream of getting a record-breaking transfer.

Now the riches and fame on offer can make players of today global superstars who transcend sport and are famous celebrities in their own right.

The glory and fame, the rush and excitement are powerful incentives to make kids dream of becoming the next Lionel Messi or Cristiano Ronaldo. The pitfalls, agents, bad advice and excitement are all part of the journey and yet it is all worthwhile if that wide-eyed youngster realises his dream of becoming a professional footballer.

It cannot be a coincidence that some of the best managers didn't have notable playing careers. The prime examples are Jose Mourinho and Arsène Wenger. Their drive and success probably came from the fact they came from little, did not have fortunes in their bank account, and their managerial career was their whole life. They needed that to succeed. They needed the career in management.